Crime

ISSUES
(formerly Issues for the Nineties)

Volume 7

Editor

Craig Donnellan

Independence

Educational Publishers
Cambridge

First published by Independence
PO Box 295
Cambridge CB1 3XP
England

© Craig Donnellan 2000

British Library Cataloguing in Publication Data
Crime – (Issues Series)
I. Donnellan, Craig II. Series
364

ISBN 1 86168 115 1

Printed in Great Britain
The Burlington Press
Cambridge

Typeset by
Claire Boyd

Cover
The illustration on the front cover is by
Pumpkin House.

CONTENTS

Chapter One: Current Trends

Chapter Two: Young Offenders

Chapter Three: Crime Prevention

Introduction

Crime is the seventh volume in the **Issues** series. The aim of this series is to offer up-to-date information about important issues in our world.

Crime looks at current trends, young offenders and crime prevention.

The information comes from a wide variety of sources and includes:
Government reports and statistics
Newspaper reports and features
Magazine articles and surveys
Literature from lobby groups
and charitable organisations.

It is hoped that, as you read about the many aspects of the issues explored in this book, you will critically evaluate the information presented. It is important that you decide whether you are being presented with facts or opinions. Does the writer give a biased or an unbiased report? If an opinion is being expressed, do you agree with the writer?

Crime offers a useful starting-point for those who need convenient access to information about the many issues involved. However, it is only a starting-point. At the back of the book is a list of organisations which you may want to contact for further information.

*****

Big crime rise after five-year fall

By Jason Bennetto, Crime Correspondent

The Home Office is admitting that crime is on the rise after falling for five years in succession. Large increases in criminal behaviour have been recorded by police forces across the country. They are being collated by Home Office statisticians who are also forecasting that crime will continue to rise for the next few years.

Jack Straw, the Home Secretary, appeared yesterday to prepare the ground for a disclosure that crime was up. The official figures for the past year will not be published until October, but Mr Straw said that although crime 'went down for the first two years of this government; the thing is whether it's going to stay down'. He added: 'I work on the basis we have to keep our effort up and keep the crime rate down.'

Mr Straw conceded that the forthcoming figures were already expected to rise by as much as 20 per cent due to a more accurate method of counting incidents, which was introduced in the past year. But he also said it 'remained to be seen' what the trend would be this year.

Even taking the new system into account, the underlying crime rate is also expected to go up. Officials were saying privately yesterday that the rise would be significant, although not 'double digit' in percentage terms.

After overseeing a drop of nearly 8 per cent to 4.6 million reported offences in England and Wales in the year to March 1998, any increase in recorded offences will be seized on by the Government's critics as evidence that current anti-crime measures are failing. A rising crime rate during the run-up to the next general election would be a major blow for Labour, which has continued to campaign on being 'tough on crime and the causes of crime'.

The Metropolitan Police, one of the few forces to disclose statistics so far, revealed that crime rose 15 per cent, to a total of 270,000 offences in May, June and July, compared with the same period the previous year.

In the West Midlands the number of reported crimes rose by 18 per cent to 315,000 for the year ending April 1999. Chief Constable Edward Crew has blamed changes in the way the Home Office records crime for much of the increase. The biggest rise, however, was in categories unaffected by the new counting system – drugs trafficking rose by 19 per cent, and wounding and assaults were up 12 per cent.

In a reappraisal of previous thinking, Home Office statisticians are also predicting that Britain's booming economy and a surge in the number of young men is expected to push up the crime rate further. A report, circulated to chief constables, forecasts that property crime could rise by up to 40 per cent within the next three years.

The new crime model takes into account a rise in birth rates since a slump in the mid-seventies. That would mean a new generation of young people reaching criminal maturity.

Experts say they now believe that a successful economy has a bad long-term effect on crime. During a boom an initial 'feel-good' period, which sees the number of offences drop as people earn more, is replaced with a crime spate as the number of valuable goods, such as cars and computers, increases and thieves have more opportunities to make easy cash.

While the Government and police have been successful in reducing property crime, particularly burglary and car theft, they have failed to stem a rise in violent and sexual offences.

To show the importance placed on winning the fight against crime, Mr Straw announced yesterday that he and his Home Office ministers are to visit 13 towns and cities across England and Wales over the next month to examine the progress of crime-fighting partnerships involving police, councils and other organisations.

© The Independent
August, 1999

The rise of Crime plc

Britain's third largest industry makes an estimated £50bn a year from illegal activities. As a report next week reveals, its most powerful leaders are not on the list of usual suspects. Tony Thompson investigates

Organised crime is now Britain's third-largest industry – worth a staggering £50 billion a year. Amid fears that police are losing the battle to curb gangsters involved in everything from drug smuggling to murder, the National Criminal Intelligence Service's annual report next week will make grim reading.

In a bid to crack down on this underworld, Special Branch, which for more than 100 years has been in the front line against terrorism and political crime, is to join forces with mainstream CIDs and begin investigating crimes such as drug smuggling and protection rackets.

Special Branch detectives, who have spent their careers investigating spies and Irish and Middle Eastern terrorists, will work with highly-trained special surveillance teams – whose most notable success in recent years was the tracking of an IRA gang trying to blow up London's electricity supply stations – to target the underworld's leading figures.

The NCIS report is expected to show that the true picture of organised crime in Britain, and London in particular, is very different from the popular image portrayed by the media. Infamous and publicly known groups such as the Yardies, the Russian Mafia and the Hell's Angels, though far more commonly written about, sit quite far down the pecking order compared with the many other gangs who quietly run their powerful empires without an unhelpfully high public profile.

For those in the know, none of this comes as a surprise.

As London 'face', Dodgy Dave Courtney, whose autobiography is published later this month, put it: 'Anyone can pull out a gun and shoot someone but real organised crime is about making money. And lots of it.

'You only get caught if you're making mistakes or drawing attention to yourself. The most successful criminals are people you never get to hear about.'

Gangs that make a killing

Traditional London 'family' gangs
Though the majority of their exploits generally fail to make the headlines, the gangs that have grown up out of the traditional London crime families are by far the most active players in today's underworld.

They dabble in protection rackets, bootlegging and some extortion, but mostly deal in drugs. Not only are they willing to deal in any drug, they will also deal with gangs of any ethnic background if the deal is good enough. Armed robbery, long seen as the traditional way to acquire the 'stake' money to buy your way into your first drug deal, has declined in recent years. Rather than an organised, experienced team of villains, most bank and cash van jobs are now carried out by loners who often have weapons which are incapable of firing. But these crimes are now making a comeback. As with all gangs operating at present, increasing prison terms and the risk of forfeiture of the criminals' cash and property mean they are slowly moving away from high-risk, high-profit activities such as drug smuggling to areas which offer high profit for far smaller risk such as fraud.

Turkish gangs
Currently responsible for more than 90 per cent of the heroin trade and working mostly from north London, the Turkish Mafia is a series of small, tight-knit cells that are notoriously difficult for police to penetrate. They link up with other UK gangs only when the product is in the country.

Turkish is a generic term – many are Cypriot or Kurdish and object to being described as anything else. Although drugs are their main activity, the Turkish gangs make use of the same smuggling and distribution networks to move large numbers of illegal immigrants and stolen vehicles. Profits are laundered though large numbers of complex transactions, often through Turkish and Cypriot banks.

So far this year there have been more than a dozen major trials involving Turkish nationals arrested for heroin smuggling. Although there is relatively little violence associated with their activities there have been a number of murders revolving around disputes between rival gangs. Customs and police officers alike confess a sneaking admiration for the Turkish gangs, particularly their organisation and their skill in concealing drugs within vehicles.

West African organised crime groups

Across the UK, the activities of these groups – mostly from Nigeria – are worth around £3bn each year. The principal fraud is known as 419 after the article of Nigerian law which it breaches.

Typically a letter arrives at the headquarters of a successful British business from someone purporting to be a senior Nigerian government official. He wants to transfer some funds out of his country and needs a UK bank account to deposit the cash in. In return for allowing the money to be paid into the account, the recipient can keep 25 per cent of the total amount which often runs to millions of pounds. For those who are fooled by the scam, the crunch comes when they hand over their account details and sample signatures to allow the transfer to take place. Instead of money being paid in, the documents and details are used to empty the bank accounts of whatever they may have contained. On average, victims lose between £50,000 and £100,000 though in some cases losses have been as high as £1m.

Recent reports from Japan show that increasing numbers of Nigerians are travelling to the country and getting married to Japanese women. With immigration status confirmed, they then forge links with the Japanese Yakuza who, because of their expertise in the field of advance fee fraud, have proved natural allies. The Yakuza has a small but growing presence in Colindale, north London, where they monitor their gang's activities throughout Europe.

Chinese criminal gangs

Although inevitably described as Triads, whether or not these gangsters are members of the Chinese secret societies, the police now acknowledge that London is increasingly being targeted by criminals from mainland China. They carry out the same sorts of crime as the traditional Triads.

At present, the chief activity of all the gangs is the trafficking of illegal immigrants. Unemployment and poverty in the People's Republic have boosted the number of people willing to pay up to £15,000 for the 'premium' smuggling service, which includes a passport, transport tickets and a job at the other end. Often the 'job' ends up with the hapless traveller being an enforcer for a London-based Triad gang. The gangs are also involved in counterfeit credit cards and fraud.

At the recent trial of a group of gangsters in a football match-fixing scam, it emerged that the London-based middle-man was a convicted fraudster with links to Triad gangs. Wai Yuen Liu lived in the home of the wife of a major Triad criminal being held in Hong Kong over a betting fraud. Yan Ming Suen, reputed head of the Wo On Lok Triad, was arrested in connection with an operation to coincide with the start of the World Cup. His wife and two young children remain in their Kensington home. Liu was jailed for five years in 1990 for a credit-card conspiracy involving 24 other suspected Triads. More than 60 cloned or stolen cards and £50,000 cash were found in his house. In 1994, Liu was acquitted of an attempted murder charge at the Old Bailey.

Colombian crime groups

Although the amount of cocaine available in the capital continues to grow and shows no sign of slowing, the Colombian drug cartels have relatively little direct contact with their product. A handful of representatives occasionally visit Britain to make contacts or oversee deliveries but mostly they keep themselves well away from the danger zone.

In rare cases where they do base themselves here, they keep as low a profile as possible. That was certainly the case with the Goldsworthy family who, despite living in their plush Fulham home for more than three years, were barely known by their neighbours. Then, one December, a few months after her husband had taken a job in the United States, Claudia Goldsworthy and her young daughters disappeared. When the police came looking they found a domestic *Marie Celeste*: furnishings and clothes all in place, food in the fridge, and schoolbooks on the kitchen table.

Neighbourhood concern rapidly turned to astonishment when those who had lived close by learnt they had been fed a string of lies. Keith hadn't gone to work abroad: he'd been sentenced to 22 years for his part in a multi-million-dollar cocaine ring. Colombian-born Claudia vanished six days before she was due to appear at Knightsbridge Crown Court charged with laundering millions of pounds of her husband's drug profits.

Indian/Pakistani groups

Rather like the traditional London gangs of old, these groups are very much family-based. This makes them difficult for police to penetrate and vastly reduces the possibility for 'turning' one member of a gang against the others.

With the advantage of equally strong links abroad, the gangs are active in the field of heroin smuggling and illegal immigration.

Violence periodically flares up between rival groups. Last week, five youths were stabbed and beaten with baseball bats in the latest tit-for-tat battle between rival Bangladeshi gangs working with stolen credit cards. Teenage gang members in the East End will regularly hire luxury sports cars using stolen licences to impress their friends. The market for the cards and licences that go along with them is lucrative, competitive and occasionally fiercely disputed.

Yardies

With 14 killings in north-west London alone this year, the activities of the Yardies have dominated the headlines. Surprisingly, the National

Criminal Intelligence Service does not have a specialist team investigating their activities.

The NCIS looks only at serious and organised crime and while the Yardies fall into the former category, few would argue that they could be seen to qualify for the latter. Many of the deaths result from disputes between relatively small organisations rather than mass warfare. However, alarmed by the number of deaths, the NCIS is looking at the Yardie problem again to see whether it warrants further attention.

The Russian mafia

Again, widely written about because of the large sums of money involved but the Russian Mafia does not have a significant physical presence in London.

Plenty of well-known 'mafioski' have visited the capital, and there is evidence of some buying up expensive property, but the influx has been nothing like what was expected and the levels of violence seen in Germany and New York –

both Mafioski strongholds – have yet to be seen here. Earlier this year, three men from the Eastern Bloc were jailed for running a brothel which used exclusively Russian prostitutes. A traditional area of Russian organised crime, Eastern Bloc women now make up more than 60 per cent of all off-street prostitutes in the capital, though it is unclear exactly how involved any organised Russian gangs are in the trade.

Biker gangs

Hell's Angels, the largest biker gang movement on Earth, have expanded at a rate that rivals many of the largest companies listed in the US magazine *Fortune*'s top 500, according to the Royal Canadian Mounted Police.

'Worldwide, they are one of the fastest growing organised crime families,' said Staff Sgt Jean-Pierre Levesque of Criminal Intelligence Service, Canada's national clearing house for police data. 'Not the richest, or the most powerful, but there's no one else who spreads their wings like they do.'

In the UK, the Angels have mostly managed to avoid being linked to organised crime, despite clear evidence of involvement of chapters across Europe and America. However, links to Canada, where the Angels are currently most active, are well established. In 1985 a Canadian Angel wanted on a murder charge was found hiding in London. British Angels had provided him with accommodation and a false passport and were planning to smuggle him to France when they were raided.

In February 1995 two more Canadian Angels were jailed for 14 years following a massive cocaine swoop. Pierre Rodrigue and David Rouleau had been arrested in a suite at the London Hilton hotel. They had contacted British Angels during their time in the country and were thought to be helping to draw up plans to open new cocaine routes into Britain.

Cost of crime in shops hits a record £2bn

Crime cost Britain's shopkeepers a record sum of more than £2 billion last year, according to new figures.

A big increase in credit- and debit-card fraud, and growing investment in security measures such as closed-circuit television, are key factors in the rise – the first for six years. The British Retail Consortium's annual crime survey is being presented to a European retail security summit in London this week.

The findings show that the cost of crime in the trade – which had been falling – increased last year by £100 million from £1.38 billion to £1.48 billion. Crime prevention measures cost a further £550 million – £100 million more than in 1997. This brings the total cost to retailers to £2.03 billion.

The survey is based on responses

By Linda Jackson, Consumer Affairs Correspondent

from 44,000 shops. It shows that, while instances of violence against staff and shoplifting decreased by up to 20 per cent, other losses rose, including the amount of card fraud, which doubled to almost £60 million.

New ways of stamping out retail crime will be discussed at the conference, which will be addressed by Jack Straw, the Home Secretary, and Sir Paul Condon, the Metropolitan Police Commissioner.

Delegates from across Europe will hear how technological advances and social changes are creating new risks for retailers, who need to explore new ways of fighting terrorism, extortion, fraud and violence.

One of the security schemes under scrutiny will be the introduction of an 'intranet' computer system at the big Bluewater shopping development in Dartford, Kent, which opened recently. Details of thieves or people acting suspiciously in the centre can be passed to all retailers at the flick of a switch.

In a separate move, developers at Bluewater have hired 22 Kent police officers at a cost of £750,000 a year. It is the first time that a police force has entered such an agreement with a private contractor.

Ann Grain, director of the British Retail Consortium, said: 'Retail crime is becoming increasingly sophisticated. Effective co-ordination across the industry with the police and other authorities is a vital strategy.'

One in ten are victims of car crime

By Philip Thornton

One in 10 people was the victim of car crime last year, according to a survey that reveals an increase in thefts and break-ins. The figure compared with 9 per cent in a similar study a year ago. The survey, published yesterday, found that car crime was the lowest in the South, where 3 per cent said they had been victims, while the highest was in Lancashire.

Of those questioned, 5 per cent had had their car broken into in the past 12 months, doubling to 10 per cent in the 25–34 age-group. The survey, published as the Home Secretary, Jack Straw, urged people to intervene when they saw crime being committed, will come as a blow to the authorities. The Home Office's British Crime Survey recorded a fall of 27 per cent in attempted thefts of vehicles and a fall of 25 per cent in attempted thefts or break-ins between 1995 and 1997.

The survey by the British Vehicle Rental and Leasing Association (BVRLA) found that those most in fear of car crime were youngsters who tended to drive older cars and less secure vehicles. Almost half those aged 17 to 24 (48 per cent) feared becoming the victim of car crime. This compared with 15 per cent of those over 55. Concern was highest in the North-east (41 per cent) and Lancashire (37 per cent).

The survey also found that 92 per cent believed manufacturers should be doing more to improve vehicle security, compared with 89 per cent in the previous survey.

Freddie Aldous, BVRLA president, said: 'While the UK remains the car-crime capital of Europe, we will continue to pressurise manufacturers to make security features standard across their range of products.' According to the association, vehicle crime accounts for a quarter of UK crime and affects more than a million drivers annually. Three out of 1,000 British motorists will have their cars stolen, compared with one in 1,000 in Switzerland, said the BVRLA.

About 30 per cent of car crime is committed in car parks, where vehicles are 200 times more likely to be broken into or stolen than those parked at home. The survey was published by the BVRLA as it

> *Those most in fear of car crime were youngsters who tended to drive older cars and less secure vehicles. Almost half those aged 17 to 24 feared becoming the victim of car crime*

announced the winners of its annual vehicle security awards. Vauxhall was voted the most secure manufacturer in the super-mini and lower-medium class, while BMW took both the upper-medium and luxury and executive sector awards.

Ford was top in the light commercial vehicle section of the awards. Mercedes-Benz won the award in the heavy goods vehicle category.

A new environmental award went to the Swedish car company Volvo, as the manufacturer that could best demonstrate 'green' credentials across the entire production process. The Home Office minister Paul Boateng said: 'Motor manufacturers have made real progress in recent years in making cars more difficult to steal. Vehicle crime accounts for a quarter of all crime and must be tackled.'

© The Independent
February, 1999

Car crime

Scotland/borders
6
18

North-east
13
41

Yorkshire
10
32

East Anglia
7
24

London
10
19

South
3
10

North-west
14
37

Midlands
7
26

Wales/South-west
12
27

Key
Per cent of those surveyed who:
Suffered car crime in 1998 — 1
Fear they will be victims of car crime in 1999 — 1

Source: Opinion Business Research

Countryside in the grip of £100m crime wave

By John Steele

The National Farmers' Union mutual insurance association estimates that crime costs farmers more than £100 million a year. Vehicle theft alone, running at 30,000 vehicles a year, costs £73 million.

For some years country dwellers in many regions have felt, with some justification, that they are in the grip of a crime wave which shows little sign of abating and that the police have been either powerless to protect them, or inept.

There is compelling evidence that thieves and burglars travel from urban areas – which are now, owing partly to the widespread use of CCTV cameras, more hostile to them – to work in the countryside. In part, this makes their attacks on rural homes more difficult to detect, though police suggest this is countered by the fact that the appearance of strange people and cars in small, intimate communities is more often noted than in urban areas.

Whatever the difficulties of tracing travelling criminals, however, the bulk do not travel very far – in most cases crossing from a built-up area in one police force or division to strike in another. The number of burglars travelling long distances to prey on remote farmers or rural dwellers should not be over-estimated.

What is significant, though, is the fear and anxiety that can exist in some rural populations when the police appear to have deserted them. Much of this may be a result of a policy of many forces in recent times to close small sub-stations and concentrate staff in larger stations on fewer sites.

> **There is compelling evidence that thieves and burglars travel from urban areas to work in the countryside**

Though a similar policy has been implemented in towns and cities the geographical areas left without an apparent police presence are much larger. If a building that always had an officer in it at night is closed and locals have to suffer the frustration of ringing a regional switchboard to find a human being – often a police civilian worker – to talk to, then the feeling is that police have let them down.

Peter Gammon, the president of the Superintendents' Association of England and Wales, said: 'Police have closed down sub-stations. But they still patrol the areas, albeit from a more central situation. It is not a matter of withdrawing from the countryside.'

However, he conceded that 'there is a lower concentration of police officers in the countryside, because of the greater acreage. Therefore, sometimes, isolated properties can become vulnerable.'

Mr Gammon's comments touch on one of the most intractable problems facing police chiefs in recent years – how to convince the public that police can still protect them from crime while having fewer officers visibly involved in general patrolling. The alternative to the 'Bobby on the Beat' is 'intelligence-led' policing.

In broad terms this means dedicating your resources to where intelligence gathering tells you crime is at its worst, for example when locals report an upsurge of drug dealing at a particular spot.

Mr Gammon said: 'Police analyse crime data and if they find that there is a problem with rural crime, then they will step up their response, both in preventative work and sending out patrols.'

Fourfold rise in drug offenders over 10 years

By Nick Hopkins

The number of people convicted of drugs offences has quadrupled over the past 10 years and drug users are now responsible for a third of all theft, burglaries and street robberies, according to a report published today.

The National Association for the Care and Resettlement of Offenders said its study, *Drug Driven Crime*, showed there were compelling reasons to direct more resources into drug treatment programmes and away from conventional punishments like prison.

Analysis of research conducted in Britain, Australia and the US proved this was the best way of preventing re-offending and substantially cutting crime rates, Nacro said.

'Conventional punishments simply produce a vicious circle of crime, punishment and a rapid return to drug use,' said Paul Cavadino, Nacro's director of policy.

'Getting drug-dependent offenders into treatment programmes is by far the most effective option. For every £1 spent on drug misuse treatment, we save more than £3 associated with the costs of crime.'

The report draws together data from numerous studies to highlight the links between the soaring number of drug users and criminal activity.

One recent survey showed users in Derby, Brighton and Southwark, south-east London, were spending between £300 and £2,000 a week on drugs, with most of the cash coming from shoplifting, burglary, fraud and prostitution.

It is estimated that across England and Wales drug users raise £850m a year through 'acquisitive crime'. The cost to the victims is thought to be £2.5bn.

Nacro points to a recent Home Office study of 7,000 criminals which concluded that drug use was more significant than any other social factor – including unemployment, accommodation and alcohol –when it came to the causes of re-offending. In Dorset, 79% of offenders with a drug problem were reconvicted.

The report cites the findings of the National Treatment Outcome Research Study, funded by the Department of Health, which followed 1,100 drug users, responsible for 70,000 crimes, after they joined treatment schemes.

Researchers found that 'both drug and criminal activity dropped substantially during the early stages of treatment', and within two years the proportion of users committing property crime fell from 52% to 27%.

Statistics of a social problem

- The number of people cautioned or convicted for drugs offences rose from 26,000 in 1987 to 113,200 in 1997.
- The number of dealing offences rose from 3,900 to 14,100 in the same period.
- A recent study estimated there were 130,000 'problematic' drug users in England and Wales.
- Drug users spend between £300 and £2,000 a week on drugs and 'only a small proportion' of the money is raised legally.
- Drug users raise up to £850m a year through 'acquisitive' crime.
- One survey reported 51% of male prisoners on remand had some sort of drug dependence.
- According to prison statistics 7,174 people were serving prison sentences for drugs offences in 1997 – a 108% increase since 1987.

One study in California estimated that drug treatment courses costing $209m led to a fall in crime which saved the state $1.5bn over 12 months.

Despite the advantages of investing in such programmes, Nacro said that funding for services in Britain is 'insecure' and it claims that there are often waiting lists which discourage drug users who need immediate attention.

It wants the government to direct a greater proportion of the £1.4bn spent annually on drug issues towards providing treatment services.

'Two-thirds of the budget is spent on law enforcement and a third on prevention and education,' said a spokesman. 'There is an imbalance at the moment and we need to look at how the funds can be reallocated.'

Nacro suggests that the money spent prosecuting cannabis users should be channelled into drug treatment programmes for people with more serious problems.

Peter Glass, director of Cranstoun drug services, which provides rehabilitation facilities for drug users across the south of England, said: 'We need to concentrate on providing community based agencies for prisoners after they leave jail. Many of these organisations are completely overstretched.'

Home Office minister Lord Bassam said that the government had given the prison service an extra £50m over the next three years for drug treatment programmes and £20m had gone to police forces to develop proper referral schemes.

In a statement, he said: 'The government is only too aware of the link between drug taking and multiple offending. It has been a priority to introduce a range of measures to help tackle this vicious cycle.'

© *The Guardian*
August, 1999

Drugs and robbery behind record rise in women jailed

More women are in jail than ever before – with record numbers serving time for drug and burglary offences.

Linda Jones, the head of women's policy at the Prison Service, revealed yesterday that the number of female inmates has doubled in five years to 3,160.

But she scotched what she termed the popular 'myth' that many of them were sent behind bars for what many critics dubbed trivial offences – non-payment of fines or TV licences.

'In March, four of the 133 prisoners held for fine default were women, and none of them were jailed for non-payment of television licences,' she said.

Current research in fact showed that women are less likely than men to be sent to jail – including for offences such as shoplifting – and those that are receive shorter sentences.

Half the record rise in numbers is down to drugs – a third of inmates were sentenced for drugs offences and another third had been involved in 'drug-related' incidents. But the number of women jailed for burglary has also risen – by 18 per cent to 130.

Mrs Jones was speaking at a conference in London entitled 'The Crisis in Women's Prisons'. While admitting, however, that the rapid rise has created a challenge, she denied that the service is 'in crisis'.

The pace of growth is slowing and alternative sentences such as community drug penalties and electronic tagging can help curb it further, she said.

Research is also under way to establish what encourages women to become criminals and if they differ from male 'criminogenic factors'.

Mrs Jones said that evidence suggested that victimisation and abuse are particularly significant factors in women's offending – estimates suggest that between 50 and 90 per cent of women in jail are thought to have been abused.

One speaker, author and prison campaigner Angela Devlin, accused 'deliberately obstructive' staff of perpetuating a 'macho and bullying' culture in jails.

Half the record rise in numbers is down to drugs – a third of inmates were sentenced for drugs offences and another third had been involved in 'drug-related' incidents

---

She claimed that too many saw female prisoners as sub-human, referring to them as 'bodies'. Officers' slang degraded women and showed a lack of concern for their well-being, she said, citing the use of words such as 'slashers' for those who mutilate themselves or 'swingers' for would-be suicides.

Miss Devlin complained about the lack of educational and training opportunities. Women were offered courses in ironing, flower arranging and '100 things to do with half-a-pound of mince' rather than learning DIY or skills to help them find work.

Mrs Jones said most staff were dedicated and caring, but admitted there were some whose attitudes were not acceptable.

'That is something we must tackle,' she said.

© The Daily Mail
June, 1999

Women in prison double in 6 years

By Andrew Hibberd

A fifth of all crime is now committed by women and the number sent to prison has doubled in six years, says a Home Office report, published yesterday.

With forecasts of an increase in the age group most likely to offend, the Home Office is expecting a surge in crime, it adds.

The number of 15- to 20-year-old females, the peak age for offending, is set to rise eight per cent by the year 2005, the report said.

The crime wave would come on top of a 100 per cent rise in the number of women jailed since 1993, compared with 45 per cent for men.

The report said that the crimes for which most women were jailed were drug offences, shoplifting, fraud and wounding.

Women were less likely to receive custodial sentences, even for similar crimes, and were more likely to be cautioned, discharged or given a community service sentence.

Women were also likely to receive shorter custodial sentences than men, the authors of the report found.

● Andrew Sparrow, Political Correspondent, writes: Men are nearly twice as likely as women to be the victim of violent crime, a Home Office study has disclosed. While 3.6 per cent of women have been the victim of a serious attack, the figure for men is 6.1 per cent.

© Telegraph Group Limited, London 1999

Crimes in Scotland

Police Records and Crime Survey results

In 1998, Scottish police forces recorded 3% more crimes and 6% more offences than in 1997. However, the trend since 1992 has been downward, so that the 1998 figure for all recorded crime is 25% fewer than recorded in 1991 when crimes reported reached their highest recent point.

The following review of recorded crime figures cites the Scottish average – local trends may vary significantly from the national situation. Similarly, between categories of crime there are variations in the rate of increase and decrease. The effect of police targeting can be seen in some of the data, for example, targeting knife possession; or the differential prosecution of prostitution; or speeding offences in the national Speedwatch campaign which yielded an increase of 26% in speeding reports over the year.

Scottish Crime Survey

The Survey estimated that in 1995 just under 1 million crimes were committed against individuals and households in Scotland. This is about an 8% drop since the previous survey year of 1992. Offences against property were just over 70% of the total in the Survey compared with 85% of the police recorded crime figures.

The Survey suggests that about 1 in 4 people experienced crime; 1 in 10 had been victims more than once. Risk varied between groups of people and types of crime. For example, the elderly were least likely to experience violent street crime and young men most likely.

Between 1992 and 1995 there was an overall 5% drop (to 50%) in the proportion of crimes experienced by the people surveyed which were reported to the police.

Violent crimes (excluding sexual crimes)

There were 21,100 violent crimes recorded by the police in 1998, up 10% on the 1997 total. Violent crimes accounted for 5% of all recorded crime in Scotland over the year.

Serious assaults (a category which includes homicides) increased by 9% to 6,593: a 10% increase in robbery was recorded to a total of 5,000 incidents. The increase is attributed to bag snatching and robbery from cash machines.

'Handling offensive weapons' crimes dropped by 12% between 1996 and 1997. Several police forces ran campaigns during 1996 targeting the carrying of offensive weapons. The number of crimes recorded will have been influenced, in the short term, by that activity. In 1998, however, there was an increase of 13% in this category to a total of 6,700.

Details of the involvement of firearms in criminal activity in Scotland are available in Recorded Crimes involving Firearms in Scotland 1998.

One explanation offered for the sharp recent rise in non-sexual violence is the widespread installation of CCTV making visible acts of violence which might have previously gone unreported.

In comparison with the police record, only 3% of the sample in the 1996 Scottish Crime Survey reported an experience of violent crime. Against a background of rising violence recorded by the police to 1996, the Survey estimates show a drop of 8% in violent incidents between 1992 and 1995 in south and central Scotland.

Crimes of Indecency

Police recorded 7400 crimes of indecency in 1998. Crimes of indecency include a wide range of behaviour from rape and its attempt, indecent assault, offences related to prostitution to the more minor indecent exposure. In all these represent only 1.6% of all recorded crimes.

There has been a steady increase in the reporting of rape and indecent assault over the decade. In 1998, 613 rapes were reported in contrast to the 320 reported to the police in 1991. This may reflect greater willingness amongst victims to report such violence rather than an increase in incidents.

The Scottish Crime Surveys do not ask about sexual offences.

Vandalism and fire-raising

Acts of vandalism recorded by the police fell by 2% to 76,600 in 1998, accounting for 18% of recorded crimes. The five district councils with the highest rates of recorded

vandalism were Glasgow, Dundee, Aberdeen, Edinburgh and West Lothian. The councils with the lowest rates were Western Isles (Eilean Siar), East Renfrewshire, Stirling, Argyll and Bute, Orkney Islands, and Shetland Islands. Fire-raising offences totalled 2,500 (down 10%).

The 1996 Scottish Crime Survey reports that home and vehicle vandalism amounted to 24% of crime experienced by the people questioned.

Vandalism rates in the Surveys seem to be moving in a different direction to the police statistics. During the 1980s police data showed a rise in such offences, and the Surveys recorded a fall. The difference was greatest in 1992. Recently the counts seem to be converging, probably because the public is more willing to report incidents of this kind.

Alcohol and drugs

One of the major changes over the last decade has been the growth of drug-related offending. In 1998, 31,460 drug-related crimes (mostly possession, and possession with intent to supply) were recorded compared with 4,736 in 1987.

Of the people proceeded against for drug-possession offences in 1995, 83% related to the possession of cannabis, 14% to amphetamines, and 4% to heroin. For a more detailed discussion of issues relating to drugs and crime see the Scottish Office *Criminal Justice Bulletin* July 1998.

Drunkenness offences totalled 8,500 – a drop of 12% on the 1997. Drunk driving offences dropped 6%.

Petty assaults were up by 2% (to 50,958) mirrored by breach-of-the-peace offences which dropped 2% (to 71,700). Many of these incidents are likely to be drink-related.

Rural crime

Both police records and 1993 Scottish Crime Survey statistics show that fewer people become victims of crime in rural areas than in urban areas, although the overall pattern of crime types is similar. In 1997 the City of Glasgow had a reported crime rate of 1,448 per 10,000, followed by Aberdeen City with a rate of 1,310. At the other end of the league are Orkney Islands at 171, Western Isles at 220, and Shetland Islands at 357.

The 1996 Scottish Crime Survey found that 11% of rural households in the sample had experienced at least one household crime compared to 18-21% of households in more urban communities.

Recent research shows that, in rural areas, 39% of people surveyed said that they were worried about becoming a victim of crime, compared with 57% in towns and cities. While rural people probably worry less about crime than town dwellers, they were concerned about the behaviour of some young people, about drug and alcohol misuse and petty vandalism. Most serious crime tended to be blamed on 'awayday' criminals travelling in from other centres.

There has been a narrowing of the difference between town and country reported-crime rates. This is more likely to reflect a greater willingness by rural dwellers to report incidents, than an increase in offending.

Some crimes are specifically 'rural crimes'. These include professional poaching of salmon and deer, fly-tipping, theft from farms (particularly all-terrain vehicles), livestock theft (particularly of sheep in the Borders) and crimes against wildlife such as birds of prey.

White-collar and company crime

The scale of white-collar crime, from fiddling expenses to major corruption, is difficult to measure. Not only can it be difficult to detect but also expensive and complex to prosecute.

Of particular concern to Scotland is the issue of corporate culpability in major fatal incidents in the offshore oil industry. Headline events include the Chinook crash of 1986 (45 people killed), the Piper Alpha disaster of 1988 (167 killed), and the 11 men lost in 1992 when a Super Puma helicopter crashed off Cormorant Alpha.

In comparison to the speed and consequences of the normal criminal process, prosecutions against companies in breach of safety regulations can take years to come to court. Indeed, there has been no prosecution arising from the Piper Alpha case.

Moreover, if a company does not have a registered office in the UK it is impossible to prosecute. On conviction, the penalties imposed are usually fines which are petty in comparison to the wealth of the offending business. For example, the drilling company Arco was fined the record amount of £250K in 1993 relating to the fatal Ocean Odyssey rig blow-out five years before. However, this amounted to a mere 0.03% of the annual profits of the parent company Atlantic Richfield.

When thinking about the often trivial matters which result in imprisonment in other criminal cases, it is worth considering how culpable managers in this strategic and important industry can escape proportionate punishment. The English Law Commission recommends that a new offence of corporate killing should be introduced to cover these sorts of cases, so that management failure cannot hide behind the acts or omissions of individual employees. Another example of corporate law-breaking having a significant widespread impact is the case of the vegetable-processing company in Fife which illegally made connections with the public water supply when its own failed. The public supply became contaminated and the 700 residents of Freuchie suffered as a result. The company was prosecuted under the Health and Safety at Work Act 1974 and fined £60,000.

Companies represent about 1% of total offenders processed by the criminal justice system in Scotland. In 1997 679 companies were fined and 52 admonished or cautioned. Compensation orders were made in only two cases.

© SACRO

Public losing confidence in modern police force

By Anthony King

People are becoming increasingly disenchanted with the police, according to the latest Gallup poll for *The Daily Telegraph*.

Although public confidence in the police is far from having collapsed, the traditional bonds linking police and public show serious signs of fraying.

Officers are still regarded by most people as friendly and good at catching criminals but they are also thought to be more remote and less respectful than they used to be,

Moreover, a substantial minority of people – roughly a third – regard them as both 'dishonest' and 'racist'.

The decline in public satisfaction with the police is measurable. Ten years ago and again in the new survey, Gallup asked: In general, how satisfied or dissatisfied are you with the way the police in Britain do their job?

As the chart shows, a substantial majority of people still believe the police are doing a good job. Nevertheless, the proportion of Gallup's respondents satisfied with the force has fallen sharply – from 74 per cent in 1989 to only 58 per cent now.

> *The police's loss of reputation undoubtedly owes much to hearsay; to what people read in the papers and see on television rather than their own experiences*

The proportion who say they are 'very' satisfied with the men and women in blue has imploded – from 26 per cent a decade ago to a mere eight per cent today. The number showing dissatisfaction has risen from 12 per cent to 25 per cent.

The police's loss of reputation undoubtedly owes much to hearsay; to what people read in the papers and see on television rather than their own experiences.

Even so, as Gallup's data shows, the proportion of people 'really pleased' with the way the police have handled a case involving them or someone they know has remained roughly the same.

The portion who say they are 'really annoyed' has increased from 20 per cent to 23 per cent, almost a quarter of the population.

When ordinary citizens do encounter police officers face to face,

Britain's police then and now

Satisfaction

In general how satisfied or dissatisfied are you with the way the police in Britain do their job?

	A decade ago	Now	Change
Very satisfied	26	8	-18
Quite satisfied	48	50	+2
Not very satisfied	9	19	+10
Not at all satisfied	3	6	+3
Neither	14	15	+1

Pleasure

During the past two years have you ever been really pleased about the way a police officer has behaved towards you or someone you know, or about the way the police handled a matter in which you, were involved?

	A decade ago	Now	Change
Yes	36	38	+2
No	64	57	-7

Annoyance

During the past two years have you ever been really annoyed about the way a police officer has behaved towards you or someone you know, or about the way the police handled a matter in which you were involved?

	A decade ago	Now	Change
Yes	20	23	+3
No	80	75	-5

The good news . . .

Do these statements apply or not?

	Applies	Doesn't
Police are mainly polite and helpful	83	14
They are good at catching criminals, solving crimes	53	41
They are underpaid given the job they do	41	40

. . . and the less good

Do these statements apply or not?

	Applies	Doesn't
They are invisible: there are too few bobbies on the beat	79	19
They are too remote from the communities they serve	66	31
They treat the public with less respect than they used to	50	42

The way we view them

Do these words and phrases apply to the police in Britain today?

	Applies	Doesn't
Friendly	79	18
Part of community	56	42
Well-respected	43	56
Racist	38	55
Dishonest	31	64
Threatening	22	76

Black people, Asians

Do you think the police on the whole treat black people and Asians better or worse or much the same as they treat white people?

	All	18-34	35-44	45-64	65+
Better	5	5	4	5	7
Worse	32	38	35	31	20
Much the same	50	47	50	49	55
Don't know	13	10	10	15	17

most find them 'friendly' (79 per cent) and 'mainly polite and helpful' (83 per cent).

A clear majority, 53 per cent, also give them high marks as professionals, regarding them as being 'good at catching criminals and solving crimes'.

A large part of the problem for the police appears to lie elsewhere: in their remoteness. More than three-quarters of people, 79 per cent, believe the police are 'invisible', with too few bobbies on the beat. Almost as many, 66 per cent, reckon the police are 'too remote from the communities they serve'.

Half of Gallup's respondents also say police officers 'treat the public with less respect than they used to' and more than half, 56 per cent, think the police are no longer 'well respected'.

In addition to their perceived remoteness, doubts about police probity, though far from universal, are disturbingly widespread. Almost one in three members of the public, 31 per cent, believes the word 'dishonest' applies to the police and almost one in four, 22 per cent, believes the word 'threatening' applies.

A large part of the problem for the police appears to lie elsewhere: in their remoteness. More than three-quarters of people, 79 per cent, believe the police are 'invisible', with too few bobbies on the beat

----

Moreover, the charge that the police are racist has stuck with many people. Gallup asked: Do you think the police on the whole treat black people and Asians better or worse or much the same as they treat white people?

As the chart shows, a majority of Gallup's sample acquit police officers of racism. Fifty per cent think officers treat members of all races much the same and a further five per cent believe black people and Asians receive better treatment.

However, a large minority, 32 per cent, believe police officers deal with black people and Asians more harshly than whites, and – as the detailed figures in the chart indicate – that proportion is substantially higher among the young.

Many in the 18–24 age group, in particular, clearly suspect the motives of the force. The findings can be read two ways: showing either majority satisfaction or minority dissatisfaction However, the comparison with a decade ago suggests the police have lost a great deal of public confidence.

• Anthony King is Professor of Government at Essex University.
© *Telegraph Group Limited, London 1999*

Recorded crime statistics

England and Wales, April 1998 to March 1999

Main points

- In the twelve months to March 1999, 84 per cent of offences recorded by the police were against property; 12 per cent were violent crimes

- Offences of violence against the person showed a 10 per cent fall; however sexual offences rose by 2 per cent and robberies increased by 6 per cent.

- Both theft of vehicles and theft from vehicles fell by 2 per cent.

- Domestic burglary fell by 6 per cent, with non-domestic burglary falling by 2 per cent.

- 29 per cent of all crimes, including two-thirds of violent crimes, were cleared up during 1998/99.

- Half of all detected crimes were cleared up using a charge or summons, whilst less than one in twelve were cleared up by interviewing a convicted prisoner.

**Notifiable offences recorded by the police
12 months ending March 1999**

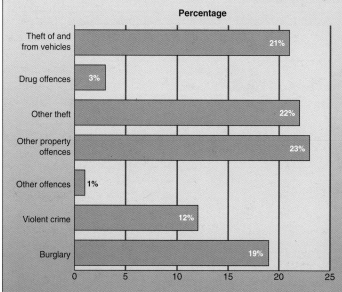

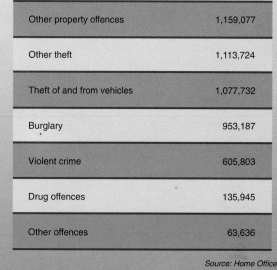

Source: Home Office

How children have changed in 50 years

By Celia Hall

Girls in Britain today are 11 times more likely to be convicted of crime than they were 50 years ago, according to a report which shows that juvenile crime overall is nearly three times higher than half a century ago.

The statistical study of the welfare of children to mark the 50th anniversary of the children's charity, the Variety Club of Great Britain, also shows that children are healthier but almost as likely to be living in poverty as they were in 1949.

The report says that the rose-tinted view of the post-war years being crime-free is untrue. In 1949 65,600 children under 17 were convicted compared with 179,300 10 to 17-year-olds in 1996. But crime rates for girls have risen dramatically. In 1949 only 4,500 of the young offenders were girls – an offending rate of 137 per 100,000 of the population. By 1996 the rate had risen to 1,500.

In 1950 commentators were attributing a 'recent rise' in juvenile crime to poor housing, neglect, family conflict and 'changing moral standards', the report says.

Jan Walsh, head of the Consumer Analysis Group, which compiled the report, said yesterday: 'The rise in female juvenile crime over 50 years is perhaps the most fascinating aspect in the report. I am sure we had not realised that equality would be measured in so many ways.

'I believe the commercial society is a root cause. There is a much greater emphasis on what we possess today. From the earliest age, through television advertising and peer pressure, children are persuaded that they must possess all kinds of things. It is now a very basic fact of a young person's life. They must have the right trainers on their feet and the right logo on their backs. This did not exist in 1949. Children made do with handed-down clothes.'

The report is based on the circumstances of 14,503,000 children under 19 in 1949 and 14,880,000 in 1999 and uses the most recent national statistics. The similar numbers are accounted for by the post-war bulge babies, mediated by number of higher infant deaths and, in the present day, by a higher chance of survival affected by contraception and abortion.

In 1949 there were nearly 35,000 deaths in under-19s in England and Wales compared with 7,000 in 1995. Fifty years ago prematurity, pneumonia, birth defects and infectious diseases took a

heavy toll. By 1995 road accidents were the commonest cause of death but, at 533, half the level of fatal road accidents suffered by children half a century ago.

The report defines poverty as households living on less than half the national average wage. It says that in the late Nineties, one in five people (18 per cent) live in poverty compared with one in four (27 per cent) in 1949. Lone parents were the most affected. Recent surveys say half of lone parents live in poverty. In 1949 divorce rates were three per 1,000 of the population. In 1995 they were 13.5.

Phillip Burley, Chief Barker at the Variety Club, which launches its annual Gold Heart day on Feb 14, said: 'Crime seems to be the new form of illness in children for which we are going to need complex social solutions. My personal view is that it is about the way we bring up children now. We give them the benefit of the doubt and enormous freedom. If everything goes well they have great advantage from this. But it's a risky policy.'

Mr Burley said it was too easy to blame the absence of fathers in many single-parent families: 'This has been the general perception for why children with lone parents do not do so well. But I think the focus is wrong and that we should be looking at the effects of poverty.'

Liz Atkins, head of public policy at the NSPCC, said: 'Hardship, unemployment and poor housing can put families under stress, which makes children more vulnerable. This report should be a spur to action to make child protection and poverty reduction the priorities of the new Millennium.'

© *Telegraph Group Limited,*
London 1999

Parents in the dock

Middle-class families are made to answer for their young tearaways

*By Graeme Wilson,
Political Correspondent*

The parents of more than 80 young offenders have been forced to take classes to make them better mothers and fathers, figures reveal today.

Couples among those handed new parenting orders are said to include several from middle-class backgrounds.

They have to take part in coaching sessions on discipline and how to communicate with adolescent tearaways.

The training also emphasises parents' responsibility to stop their children roaming the streets late at night and making sure they are not hanging around with the wrong sort of people.

Parents who refuse to comply with the orders face fines of up to £1,000.

The Home Office stressed that the orders had been imposed on a wide range of people, including affluent parents in good jobs.

'When you look at these figures, it's clear we're not just talking about the typical working-class family from the big housing estates,' said one insider.

The parenting order is one of a number of new measures unveiled in last year's Crime and Disorder Act which have been tested in ten pilot areas across England since October. Not all the pilot areas try out each initiative – only nine are using the parenting orders, for instance.

Home Office Minister Lord Bassam will announce today that, since the pilots started, 602 reparation orders have been imposed on young offenders. These force them to face up to their crime by apologising to their victims or repairing damage caused.

Courts have also issues 344 action plan orders, which include a mixture of reparation and punishment, tailored to individual youngsters.

Nine pilot areas – which include several London boroughs, Sunderland, St Helens, Sheffield, Devon, Blackburn, Hampshire and Bedfordshire – are trying out a scheme to abandon the practice of giving young offenders a string of cautions.

Instead, they face a three-stage process – a first reprimand, followed by a final warning if they commit another offence. If they break the law again, they go to court.

Today's figures show that 3,543 reprimands have been issued and 1,799 final warnings.

Home Office Minister Charles Clarke said last night that the new policies were designed to nip criminal behaviour in the bud.

'We are determined to change things for the better and do all we can to ensure that the young offenders of today do not become the career criminals of tomorrow,' he said.

'Young people who commit crimes must be made to face up to their offending behaviour and show a greater degree of responsibility to their community.

'In the pilot areas, final warnings have replaced ineffective repeat cautions, reparation orders are ensuring offenders repair the damage they do to others and parenting orders are making parents take greater responsibility for their children's behaviour.'

While the moves have been broadly welcomed by the Police Federation, the National Association for the Care and Resettlement of Offenders has questioned the targeting of parents.

In St Helens, 21 parenting orders have been imposed.

Alan Critchley, a senior member of the St Helens youth offending team, conceded that the orders are usually greeted with resentment but eventually parents recognised their value.

'For some, this has been the first practical help they have been offered in ensuring that their children keep out of trouble,' he said.

One parent said the course has been more helpful than expected.

'I have been able to discuss my son's offending behaviour with him and talk to him about what I have learnt from the course. We have been able to agree who he should hang around with and how much pocket money he should get.'

Life becomes more violent for younger men

By Cherry Norton, Health Correspondent

Life is becoming more violent for young men, who are significantly more likely to be stabbed or shot than they were 20 years ago. Figures published yesterday showed that the number of men aged 20 to 34 who are murdered rose by 51 per cent between 1979 and 1997, and by 35 per cent for men aged 15 to 44.

Older people are much less likely to be killed; 10 per million in 1997 for those over 70 years old, compared with 28 per million in 1979.

Experts believe that growing unrest among young men, who find themselves out of work with little money, and the growing availability of guns and knives, have led to the rise in the murder rate in the age group.

The report on trends in homicide, published yesterday by the Office for National Statistics, found that methods of killing have changed over the 20-year period. Cleo Rooney, author of the report, said:

'Stabbing and shooting have both increased, but shooting still accounts for only 10 per cent of recorded homicides.

'Women are more likely to be strangled or asphyxiated, while young men are more likely to be stabbed or shot.'

In 1979, 170 people were killed with sharp instruments, compared with 210 in 1997, and 35 were shot dead in 1979 compared with 60 in 1997.

Homicide is a rare cause of death in England and Wales, accounting for one in 800 deaths from injury or poisoning, but is much higher in men than women. The highest risk of being killed is for children under five years old, who tend to die from head injuries; 44 infant boys per million are murdered, and 35 per million infant girls.

Once past infancy the rate falls rapidly, and children aged 5 to 14 of both sexes have the least risk of being murdered.

An international comparison found that overall mortality rates from homicide were lower in England and Wales at 13 per million compared with the US, 88 per million, and Scotland, 22 per million. New Zealand, Israel, Australia and Canada had higher murder rates than England and Wales, but many European nations such as France, Denmark and the Netherlands had lower rates.

'The homicide rate in the USA was six and a half times that in England and Wales largely due to firearms, which reflects the enormous difference in the accessibility of guns between the two countries,' said Ms Rooney. 'Britain is higher up the international table in terms of murder rates compared with previous studies because inquest figures, where 98 per cent of the pending cases are murder, have been included,' she said.

© The Independent
August, 1999

Keeping young people away from crime

A good deal of crime is committed by young people – one-third of all known offenders are under 17. Mostly it is against property – 40 per cent of offenders dealt with for theft from shops and 35 per cent of those dealt with for burglary of premises other than dwellings were juveniles. Fortunately, most will stop offending as they grow older; but there is no need simply to wait and hope.

By following the advice in this information you, your family, your neighbours, or your business will be less likely to become a victim of juvenile crime. But it makes sense to find ways of steering young people away from crime and other anti-social behaviour in the first place. They need alternative outlets for their energy and imagination. In many areas, this point is already well recognised – by parents, teachers,

---

Fortunately, most young people will stop offending as they grow older; but there is no need simply to wait and hope

---

youth workers for example – who are working, often together, to provide these alternatives. Although its precise effects on the crime rate and people's fear of crime cannot be measured, its value in this context is not in doubt. It is supported, and sometimes provided, by Government, local authorities and the police. Charities and voluntary organisations play a major role in the provision of constructive activities for young people, for example NACRO (the National Association for the Care and Resettlement of Offenders), the Save the Children Fund, the Children's

Society and many local groups. Some schemes are funded by local authorities and the DoE together through the Urban Programme, by the Department of Education and Science via Education Support Grants or from other central government sources. But whether or not they receive help in this way, youth work schemes will only be successful if they have the goodwill and help of people in the communities where the activities are based.

If you care about young people, as well as about crime, you will want to consider how you can help. Many very worthwhile projects need sponsorship, equipment or accommodation; and may also have continual need for volunteers to work with young people, especially those who can pass on a skill or interest.

Alternatively, you may be someone who can recognise a need for some kind of activity for young people that is not available in your area. Whether acting as an individual – a young person yourself, a parent, businessman, teacher, somebody with a skill or interest or just someone with time on your hands – or as a part of a group – a Neighbourhood Watch, a Crime Prevention Panel, a Chamber of Commerce, a school – if you have an idea for something that you can do or provide, your Crime Prevention officer will be pleased to discuss it with you and advise you.

Some examples

The examples which follow are all based on projects that either exist now, or have recently been tried. It

If you care about young people, as well as about crime, you will want to consider how you can help

is worth noting that in some instances it is young people themselves who have taken the lead in organising projects:

- Some schemes, as well as offering sports or creative opportunities to those who are not attracted to formal youth clubs, provide advice on financial health, addiction or other personal problems. A school has made facilities available out of term time and local people help out as volunteers, providing support for professional workers and counsellors.
- One local authority had arranged for graffiti to be removed from its town-centre subways, while the local junior crime-prevention panel ran a competition among local schools for 'replacement' designs and murals. Local firms supplied the materials and prizes and the WRVS provided refreshments while the work was being done.
- Two high-street banks have been sponsoring a Saturday morning activities club providing a wide range of interests such as table tennis, snooker, pool, darts, weight training, basketball, a music workshop, computers and visits to areas of local importance.

- Some police forces run summer holiday activities for school children. One police force organises an annual summer holiday scheme where over 5,000 young people between 10 and 15 years old have enjoyable things to do during the summer holidays. A local bus company allows cheap fares to and from events, the programme is paid for by advertisers, and volunteers act as supervisors and helpers.
- Another force has combined with its Police Authority and local education authority to run a street football competition. The final of this competition is played at a First Division club's ground. A national bank provides sponsorship which goes towards equipment and trophies.
- The Duke of Edinburgh's Award Scheme provides a broadly based programme of activities for all young people aged between 14 and 25. It challenges them to serve others, acquire new skills, experience adventure and make new friends. The scheme operates through schools, youth organisations, industrial concerns and 'open centres' for young people who are not members of a particular organisation.

Help!

If you think you might like to help or join in activities such as these contact your Crime Prevention Officer (or your local authority youth service) who will be able to put you in touch with work already going on in your area or advise you about starting a project.

© *Neighbourhood Watch/Home Office*

Crime spree children get theft therapy

By Tony Thompson,
Crime Correspondent

Martin is the leader of a gang of highly skilled shoplifters. He draws up plans of action, issues orders in advance and carries out 'hits' with military precision.

Martin is seven years old. He has the criminal nous of somebody at least twice his age. Typically, one of his team distracts store staff while the others carry the goods out of view of security cameras and stuff them into pockets or bags. They steal to order, selling the loot to 'fences'.

'The police are too stupid to catch me,' Martin sneers. 'Besides, I'm too young. They can't do anything.'

He is one of a growing number of young children committing crimes ranging from theft and burglary to criminal damage, drug abuse and even sexual offences. Because anyone under 10 is below the age of criminal responsibility, no statistics are kept on their activities. However, police, social services and youth agencies agree that the problem is significant, and urgently needs to be addressed.

'Children are stealing from their schools and from their parents,' says Rhona Lucas, leader of the Portsmouth-based Persistent Young Offender Project.

'They are committing the same offences as adults, albeit on a smaller scale. In one case, two boys of five and six were throwing large blocks of concrete from bridges on to passing cars, and in another a seven-year-old boy was running away from home to spend time on the streets with homeless alcoholics.

'Often the parents are simply unable to control their children. And if they can't control them at six or seven, you know that for sure they are not going to be able to control them at 13 or 14 when they are bigger and stronger.'

With some youngsters progressing faster in their criminal careers than their academic ones, the fear is that they could become hooked on a life of law-breaking. Research by David Farrington, professor of psychological criminology at Cambridge University, indicates that those involved in crime before they are 14 tend to go on to become the most persistent offenders.

'Often the parents are simply unable to control their children. And if they can't control them at six or seven, you know that for sure they are not going to be able to control them at 13 or 14 when they are bigger and stronger'

But in a controversial programme aimed at breaking the cycle of crime, children such as Martin are being given counselling and social support in an attempt to challenge their behaviour.

The programme was not aimed originally at children so young. It changed when the number of extremely young offenders came to light. The project began last summer after Hampshire police found that 74 per cent of youth crime in Portsmouth was committed by only 20 people.

The offenders are as young as six. Nine of the 38 on the scheme are under 10, and half the rest are aged from 10 to 12.

The younger ones are assigned mentors, who sit with them at school every afternoon. Rewards tailored to each child, such as trips to amusement parks, are earned by a period of going straight.

'It's what middle-class parents in more affluent families do all the time,' says Lucas.

There are fears that the reward system might encourage other children to offend to gain the same benefits – a phenomenon seen when young criminals were taken on exotic safaris as part of their 'punishments'.

'Our incentives have to be earned through non-offending,' says Lucas. 'And we take the siblings of those on the programme away on treats to ensure they don't feel they are missing out.'

Those aged between 10 and 12 are treated a little differently. Eight of them will soon be taken on an overnight camping trip, and assigned tasks to build their team skills. The group will also be subjected to 'shock' lectures from prison officers describing the grim realities of life in jail.

'It might seem a little harsh,' says Lucas, 'but when you see their level of knowledge about their offending, their view that they are untouchable and that what they are doing is big and clever, it seems justified.

'They are very switched on. They know they can offend with impunity.'

The Portsmouth scheme is experimental, but this week, Home Office Minister Paul Boateng will visit the project to see whether it should be expanded nationwide as crime by children grows. A scheme targeting children as young as eight is to begin in central Scotland this month.

© The Guardian
April, 1999

Youth courts told to use powers to 'name and shame'

Magistrates yesterday received a stiff rebuke from the Home Secretary, Jack Straw, for failing to use powers they have had for more than nine months to 'name and shame' persistent teenage offenders.

Mr Straw faced criticism from penal reformers for pressing ahead with the plan, saying it would lead to the media hounding of teenagers and may in some cases backfire, by turning young offenders into 'heroes' among their friends.

But the Home Office Minister, Alun Michael, said the move would help to 'open up the "secret garden" of the youth court' and criminals could no longer hide behind the cloak of anonymity.

'Victims very rarely see what happens in court. And for far too many years youngsters have been spectators. They have been processed through the courts rather than being made to face up to the consequences of their action.'

Mr Michael said that previous practice had placed too much emphasis on protecting the identity of young offenders at the expense of victims and the community.

The power for youth court magistrates to order that criminals as young as 10 may be named in the media was put on the statute book by the former Home Secretary, Michael Howard, in his

By Alan Travis, Home Affairs Editor

Crime (Sentences) Act. The powers were implemented last September, but it is clear from the decision to issue new Home Office guidance yesterday that few magistrates have used them.

Court officials have already expressed fears that there might be appeals to the crown court in about half the cases in which orders are made to lift anonymity. It is estimated that these appeals alone could cost a further £4 million and lead to delays at a time when the Government is committed to halving the time it takes to deal with a young offender in the courts.

> **Naming could also be allowed 'where alerting others to the young person's behaviour would help to prevent further offending'**

The new guidance, issued jointly by the Home Office and Lord Chancellor's Department, says youth courts should consider allowing defendants to be named 'where the nature of the offending is so serious or persistent that it has impacted on a number of people, or his or her local community in general'.

Naming could also be allowed 'where alerting others to the young person's behaviour would help to prevent further offending'.

The guidance also reminds the youth courts that all victims should have the opportunity to attend trials unless it is against the interests of justice.

Paul Cavadino, of the National Association for the Care and Resettlement of Offenders, welcomed the idea of allowing the victims of crime to attend previously closed youth court hearings, but voiced serious concerns about 'naming and shaming' juveniles.

'This is a retrograde step. The reason why the names of young offenders are not normally published is that it can seriously damage their rehabilitation. They way the media have hounded a few young offenders named after crown court trials, sometimes for years afterwards, shows how important the rule of anonymity is.'

Mr Cavadino said some repeat delinquents revelled in the notoriety. 'Naming them in the press could have the unfortunate effect of making them heroes amongst their friends.'

I SENTENCE YOU TO CONTINUAL MEDIA SCRUTINY, STIGMATISATION, DIFFICULT EDUCATION AND EMPLOYMENT PROSPECTS - NOT TO MENTION REHABILITATION....

- DON'T USE SO MANY **BIG** WORDS - I'm ONLY TEN...

Juvenile leads

A little listening can go a long way in helping young people in prison. Lynne Wallis reports

The surroundings are more reminiscent of holidays than punishment, but the high security is grimly evident inside, and it becomes clear this isn't somewhere any 16-year-old would ever choose to be. Portland young offenders' institution (YOI), a 200-year-old cluster of buildings where convicts bound for Australia once earned their fares breaking rocks, sits right on the Dorset coast near Weymouth.

It is home to about 550 young offenders aged 15 to 21 – around 200 are under 18 – and also a new National Association for the Care and Resettlement of Offenders (Nacro) pilot project, where they have installed paid mentors inside the prison to befriend juveniles (15 to 17s) and help them to lead useful lives on release.

Prisoner mentoring until now has been delivered on a voluntary basis, by those with good intentions and sufficient free time on their hands to become prison visitors. But the Portland project, which is being funded by the Monument Trust for three years and began in January, is the first time paid mentors have been used.

Richie Dell, one of two mentors at Portland, works with 15 juveniles at a time. He was formerly a prison officer at Portland, disillusioned by the lack of sufficient resources to rehabilitate young inmates.

Sporting a 1950s quiff, brothel creepers and a permanent Woodbine, Dell has the respect of the inmates he helps, but his previous experience within the prison means he's no walkover. He says: 'Some are 15, still children, with no hair on their faces and unbroken voices. They seem so innocent, and then you learn they've been terrorising entire neighbourhoods.'

Dell chats informally on a constant basis with the offenders, in his office, their cells or in the pool table area, rather than having 'sessions'. He earns their trust and gets them talking about their various histories, problems and feelings. 'It's only when you know about their pasts that you can continue to work on their futures,' he explains. He and his colleague, Roy Koerner, a former youth worker, help with practical things like job and training applications and housing, but they work on mental processes too, such as victim empathy. One youth blinded someone in a knife attack, and Dell encouraged him to keep his hand over his eye to develop empathy for his victim. 'Never mind that you feel silly,' he was told. 'Imagine how your victim feels.'

> **'Some are 15, still children, with no hair on their faces and unbroken voices. They seem so innocent, and then you learn they've been terrorising entire neighbourhoods'**

They also try to involve families in the process and inevitably find themselves helping to resolve conflicts. Dell says: 'One lad, David, had an unhealthy respect for a law-breaking stepbrother, and we worked on that, slowly taking apart his suitability as a role model.' With Dell's help, he has applied for a place at catering college on release, and is due out of Portland in two weeks.

David says: 'At first, I didn't know what Richie's job entailed, so I gave him a bit of attitude. Then I heard he only accepted 50% of the inmates who apply to be helped, and I got interested. Now, I speak to him as freely as I do my social worker, but I only see her twice a month.'

Most juveniles are under the social services remit rather than probation, but visits from either are infrequent due to travel costs and time pressures.

Dell arranged a drug-awareness programme for David, who has been drug-free for several months, and he says the help he's received has made him more open-minded and outgoing. He adds: 'I want to be friends with the kind of people outside who just like a beer at weekends, and I want to make my family proud of me again.' He will be encouraged to keep in contact with Dell when he's released, and every effort will be made to find a mentor in his community.

A staggering 80% of all young offenders under 16 commit further offences within two years. Portland is one of just four YOIs in the country holding so many juveniles, and its inmates have more acute problems than most others – the majority have been excluded from school, 90% abuse alcohol or drugs, and 30% have been in some form of institutional care. One of the scheme's architects, Dennis Valentine, says: 'Juveniles have different needs because they are so vulnerable, compliant and easily influenced. We'd like to see juveniles moved right out of the prison system because they need more support than it can offer.'

Justin, 17, is serving three years for armed robbery, although he was hiding in a field when the robbery took place. The gun belonged to his ex-army brother. With Koerner's help, Justin is applying for a place on a carpentry and joinery course. 'I've built a relationship with Roy now,' he says. 'They work on making a bond with their clients, and you can confide in them. He's more experienced in life than I am, whereas a probation officer just checks up on you.'

Risk of experiencing crime in Scotland

Information from SACRO

Young people

The 1996 Scottish Crime Survey study of 353 teenagers aged 12–15 found that:

- 20% had been victims of theft, mostly of items that had been left unattended at school;
- 24% had been victims of a violent incident, most of which were started by youngsters of a similar age known to the victim, or previously seen by them;
- young people are more likely than older adults to experience annoying, upsetting or frightening harassment, such as being followed, or having abusive comments made at them or witnessing indecent exposure: in the 16-24 age group, 34% had such experiences (whole sample 14%, people over 65, 5%);
- young people tended to be reluctant to report incidents to adults, particularly the police – only about 13% of young victims of theft or violence reported crimes to the police;
- nearly a third of the young victims said that they had committed an offence, and 28% said that they had done so during the last year.

Violence, house-breaking and car theft

The likelihood of being a victim of violence is influenced by age, sex, social group, and leisure time spent out of the house.

The 1996 Scottish Crime Survey found that in relation to violence:

- only 3% of people surveyed had suffered a violent incident;
- 10% of young men in the 16 to 24 age group had been victims of violence and risk was greatest for young men living in high crime areas who spend more evenings away from home;
- 17% of incidents happened in pubs or discos;
- 30% of the incidents experienced by women were domestic compared with 3% experienced by men;
- 56% of incidents took place between 6pm and midnight.

The Crime Surveys do not include questions about sexual crimes.

Only 3% of households in the 1996 Scottish Crime Survey had experienced an attempted or actual house-breaking during the previous year, although a minority (11%) had suffered repeated break-ins. Risks were highest in:

- high crime areas;
- accommodation rented from council or housing associations;
- tenements or flats;
- for single-adult households;
- for people with lower levels of disposable income;
- both the lowest and the highest socio-economic groups;
- in settlements with a population between 10,000 and 99,000.

There was a significant emotional impact in most cases. For over half of those interviewed in the 1993 Scottish Crime Survey, the worst thing about the incident was the 'invasion of privacy'. Loss of possessions was the 'worst thing' for only 8% of the sample.

The 1993 Scottish Crime Survey estimates that 1 vehicle-owning household in 5 across Scotland was affected by vehicle crime in 1992. Households at highest risk were those:

- parking on the street;
- living in rented accommodation;
- in high crime areas;
- in densely populated areas;
- with higher levels of income and conversely, with lower levels of income.

- The above is an extract from the web site www.sacro.org.uk

© SACRO

My thoughts on teens, crime, and the community in Japan

Crime now

In Japan recently, there has been a growing sense of crisis about crime in communities, especially by teenagers. The major crime issues Japanese teenagers face now are substance abuse (alcohol, drugs, and tobacco) which often started out of curiosity, sexual abuse of high school students, robbery, larceny, shoplifting, purse snatching, homicide (murder) and suicide. Gang crimes have not been the top-ranked community problem. Japan is an island, which means that it is more difficult to have gang influence from other countries. In addition, possessing firearms is strictly prohibited in Japan. That is one way we have maintained our safety.

In our communities, teenagers can easily get drugs from some foreign sellers. And a few girls in high schools commit prostitution just because they want to have 'easy' money. Suicide is a major problem for teenagers. It happens a lot. The most serious fear of Japanese teenagers is impulse killing. Currently there is a school environment in which teens possess butterfly knives to defend themselves from bullying. Teens have sometimes killed persons with these butterfly knives. Even in Japan, if a woman walks alone or on a dark and deserted street at night, she could be in danger of being victimised, or even raped, though this does not happen very often.

Crime prevention

Now, for some people, crime has become a worry in Japan. How can crime be prevented before someone becomes a victim? In some high schools, the teachers suggest the following things:

- You should report where you go and have a contact phone number with you for your parents or someone you trust.

By Keiko Suzuki,
Student, Japan

- Don't take a part-time job unless you are really having difficulties in having enough money.
- If you have a date with a boy friend, you should date with some other friends and at a safe place.
- Have courage to just say 'NO' to your friends who induce you to criminal behaviour.
- Take responsibility for your belongings in school. For example, you should carry your valuables with you when you go out of your homeroom.
- Follow school discipline. For instance, put on your school uniform, don't put on accessories, don't dye your hair when you are in school.

Education about crime

In actuality, crime prevention education is very limited. Besides, most teachers don't have confidence in dealing with crime situations or students who commit crime. So there are some organisations who make up for the crime prevention elements not taught in school. For example, there is a crime hotline where you can talk with a professional counsellor by phone. It is better for you because a student doesn't have to tell who he or she is. However, there is

With the crime rate in Japan increasing now, education about crime prevention is an absolute necessity

also a few non-profit associations like Boys & Girls Clubs of America for Japanese youth.

Who prevents crime?

In general, police officers in the neighbourhoods keep them safe by patrolling the city. But in Japan, there is no one like the school resource officers who work in some schools in America. So if the criminal behaviour was committed by students in a school, their teachers would have to deal with it. There are some police boxes (the *koban*) in the neighbourhoods, but the police aren't always there. So it is important that the teenagers' families or teachers help keep an eye on them.

Why is there so little crime in Japan?

Japanese have a kind of consciousness of the shame of committing a crime. If it is proved you commit a crime, you and even your family would never be involved in your community. As most of the Japanese are afraid of that, they even hesitate to confront or argue with other people. It means that it is important for them to be a part of their communities.

The youth are the future!

Some of the youth feel the necessity of stopping crime in their communities. But there are fewer children who really think so than there are in America because most of them don't feel they are in danger. With the crime rate in Japan increasing now, education about crime prevention is an absolute necessity. And it should be done for every child regardless of their having interest in it or not.

- All opinions expressed above are Ms Suzuki's own.

What do you know about teens as crime victims?

Information from the US National Crime Prevention Council

The following questions and answers are based chiefly on information from an annual survey of the nature of and extent to which citizens and particular groups of citizens are victimised by crime. Material is also drawn from a special report, *Teenage Victims: A National Crime Survey Report*. The surveys and the special report are compiled and published by the Bureau of Justice Statistics, Office of Justice Programs, US Department of Justice.

1. In which age category are persons most likely to be victims of crime?
a. the elderly (65 and over)
b. middle-aged people (35-49)
c. teenagers (12-19 years old)

2. If you are 12 years old, what is the approximate risk that you will be a victim of violent crime during your lifetime?
a. 1 in 2 (50%)
b. 5 in 6 (83%)
c. 2 in 3 (66%)

3. Are teenage males or females more likely to be victims of violent crime?
a. males
b. females
c. males and females are equally likely

4. For the three violent crimes of rape, robbery, and assault, are teens more likely or less likely to be victimised by persons they know than are adults?
a. less frequently victimised by someone they know than are adults
b. more frequently victimised by someone they know than are adults
c. victimised by someone they know at about the same rate as adults

5. Of the violent crimes of homicide, rape, robbery, and assault, which is the most likely to be committed by a stranger?
a. homicide
b. rape
c. robbery
d. assault

6. Of the violent crimes of homicide, rape, robbery, and assault, which is the most likely to be committed by someone the victim knows?
a. homicide
b. rape
c. robbery
d. assault

7. What are the two leading causes of injury-related death among people under 20? (check two)
a. suicides
b. homicides
c. motor vehicle crashes

8. What fraction of rape victims are teenagers?
a. one-tenth
b. one-third
c. one-half

9. Which of the following age groups is least likely to report a crime?
a. the elderly (65 and older)
b. teenagers (12-19 years old)
c. middle-age groups (35-49 years old)

10. What share of violent crimes against teens occurs on the street, park or playground?
a.   1 of 3 (33%)
b.   1 of 8 (12%)
c.   1 of 2 (50%)

Quiz answers (and harder questions)

1. In which age category are persons most likely to be victims of crime?
c. Teenagers (12-19 years old). Teenagers are crime's most frequent target. Teens are victims of violent crime and crimes of theft at about twice the rate of the adult population (age 20 and older). Younger teens (12-15 years old) had lower violent crime and theft rates than older teens (16-19). (Source: *Criminal Victimization in the United States*, 1992, US Department of Justice)

... WHICH IS THE MOST DANGEROUS NEIGHBOURHOOD AROUND HERE?

—TEENAGERHOOD...

Why are teens victims of crime more frequently than any other age group? Among the reasons most frequently offered are that teens:

- have a lifestyle that puts them in locations where there is more crime and at times when there is more crime;
- are more trusting and naive and more easily led into vulnerable situations;
- are not even aware sometimes that a crime has been committed against them;
- don't know about or can't find positive activities and thus hang around dangerous situations;
- are close to other teens, and the teen population has a higher percentage of offenders than other age groups;
- are subject to negative peer pressure;
- have more difficulty in resolving conflicts without violence;
- are not well-integrated into or protected by the community;
- may have been abused and conditioned to use violence;
- suffer from lack of good role models;
- do not report crime as frequently and, as a result, victimisation continues;
- feel loyalty to family even in illegal situations;
- have families that don't care;
- feel they may not be believed;
- fear retaliation; and
- feel invincible.

2. If you are 12 years old, what is the approximate risk that you will be a victim of violent crime during your lifetime?

b. 5 in 6 (83%). Someone who is 12 years old has a 5 in 6 (83 per cent) chance of being a victim of violent crime during his or her lifetime. And 50 per cent of all victims will be victims more than once. (Source: *Lifetime Likelihood of Victimization*, US Department of Justice, March 1987)

What kinds of things can be done to reduce the number of teenagers who are victims of crime? Among the most frequent responses:

- Make teens aware of the crime risks they face.

- Educate teens about avoiding and preventing crime.
- Get parents more involved in the activities and safety of teens.
- Organise the community to make it safer.
- Sponsor more positive activities for teens.
- Build teen self-esteem and pride.
- Build better relationships between teens and law enforcement.
- Build life skills of teens, including decision making and problem solving.
- Make laws to make it tough for weapons, especially guns, to be used by or against teens.
- Involve teens in improving the community.
- Focus more media attention on teen accomplishments.
- Provide more resources for the needs of teens.

3. Are teenage males or females more likely to be victims of violent crime?

a. Males. Like their adult counterparts, teenaged males have higher violent and theft crime rates than do females. (Source: *Teenage Victims*, US Department of Justice, 1991)

What might account for teen males being more frequent crime victims? Among the reasons that have been indicated are:

- Teenage male offenders are much more likely to victimise other teen males.
- Male teens are much more likely to become involved in risky situations in which the law intervenes.
- In most societies, males are more likely than females to be offenders and victims.

4. For the three violent crimes of rape, robbery, and assault, are teens more likely or less likely to be victimised by persons they know than are adults?

b. More frequently victimised by persons they know than are adults. Teenagers are more likely to be victimised by people they know than adults. The proportion of violent crime victims who have reported that their offenders are known to them (casual or close acquaintances, friends, relatives) is 36 per cent for

young adults, 38 per cent for older teenagers (aged 16-19), and 52 per cent for younger teenagers (aged 12-15). (Source: *Criminal Victimization in the United States*, 1992)

What does this suggest? The image of the offender as a stranger – an unknown person who unexpectedly strikes – is incorrect. Too often the offender is someone who is very much like us. Much crime arises out of personal disputes where someone does not know how to handle anger or how to get away from a potentially dangerous situation.

What kinds of things can teens do to decrease crime among people who know each other? To reduce crime among teens who know one another, teens could:

- learn how to deal with their anger in non-violent ways;
- learn to communicate well, so that misunderstandings will not lead to violence;
- install conflict resolution classes and mediation programs in the school and/or community; and
- promote a general ethic of not settling disputes by violence or coercion – through posters, buttons, education campaigns, etc.

5. Of the violent crimes of homicide, rape, robbery, and assault, which is the most likely to be committed by a stranger?

c. Robbery. Robbery is the violent crime most likely to be committed by a stranger. In 1992, more than 80 per cent of robberies (against all victims, not just teens) were by strangers, compared with 46 per cent of rapes and 56 per cent of assaults. Males are more likely to be victims of all types of violent crime (with the exception of rape) by strangers than are females – 89 per cent of robberies by strangers, compared to 65 per cent for females. (Source: *Criminal Victimization in the United States*, 1992)

Why do you think robbery is the violent crime most likely to be committed by a stranger? One possible reason that robbery is the most likely to be committed by a stranger has to do with the intent of the crime. Robbery is more often premeditated – that is, the offender has the intention of committing the crime for some time before he or she commits it and is looking for a good target. In a high percentage of other violent crimes, the crime occurs after two or more persons who know one another become involved in a dispute.

6. Of the violent crimes of homicide, rape, robbery, and assault, which is the most likely to be committed by someone the victim knows?

a. Homicide. Homicide is the violent crime in which the victim is most likely to know the offender in some way. According to the *Uniform Crime Reports* for 1993 (this report includes only crime that is reported to police), almost half of the murder victims in 1992 were related to (12 per cent) or acquainted with (35 per cent) their assailants. Among all female murder victims in 1993, 29 per cent were slain by husbands or boyfriends. Three per cent of the male victims were killed by wives or girlfriends. Arguments resulted in 29 per cent of the murders in 1990.

What are some ways to prevent homicide between those who know one another? Some people feel that homicide is not a very preventable crime, but some things can be done to stop conflict before it gets to the point of violence:

- Teach people to walk away from a dispute if the parties become too angry.
- Teach people to stay away from alcohol and other drugs, because their use is associated with people becoming murderers or victims.
- Get people who are either abusers or the victims of violence to get help to stop that violence or to break off the relationship.
- Have community resources to treat the mentally ill.

7. What are the two leading causes of injury-related death among people under 20? (check two)

b. and c. According to the National Center for Health Statistics, injury was the leading cause of death for youth below age 20 in 1991. Homicide was second only to motor vehicle crashes as the leading cause of fatal injuries. Two in 5 injury deaths of these youth in 1991 were the result of motor vehicle collisions. More than 1 in 5 injury deaths

resulted from homicide. Between 1986 and 1991, while the number of youth dying in motor vehicle crashes declined 20 per cent, homicide deaths rose substantially. (Source: *National Center for Health Statistics*, US Department of Health and Human Services, 1991)

How would you convince other teens to do things to reduce their risk of injury? Some of the things teens can do to convince other teens to reduce injury risks are:

- Help other teens to picture possible short-term and long-term results of injury.
- Carry out awareness campaigns using posters, announcements, articles in the newspaper, etc.
- Set up support groups (like Students Against Driving Drunk) that emphasise preventing serious injury.

8. What fraction of rape victims are teenagers?

b. One-third. Women aged 16 to 24 were three times more likely to be raped than other women. The average annual rate of completed and attempted rape from 1973 to 1987 for women aged 12-15 was 2.3 per 1,000; for women aged 16-19, 4.8 per 1,000; and for women aged 20-24, 4.1 per 1,000. (Source: *Report to the Nation on Crime and Justice*, Second Edition, US Department of Justice, 1990)

Are there ways to help rape victims? If so, what are they? Ways to help rape victims include:

- urging the victim to report the crime to police;
- just being there to listen and to indicate that you want to help; and
- pointing out or finding out about places to go for professional help.

9. Which of the following age groups is least likely to report a crime?

b. Teenagers (12-19 years old). Teenagers are the age group least likely to report crime. Crimes against teenagers are less likely to be reported to the police than crimes against adults. In 1992, persons aged 12 to 19 reported only 24 per cent of the crime in which they were victimised. (Source: *Criminal Victimization in the United States*, 1992)

Why do teenagers report crime less often than adults? How could we encourage teens to report crimes more often? Among the reasons teens don't report crime:

- incident not considered important enough;
- embarrassment at being a victim of crime;
- desire to retaliate and 'settle a score' without reporting;
- fear of retaliation;
- ignorance of the channels for reporting;
- the feeling that nothing will happen as a result of the report; and
- poor relationship between teens and law enforcement.

10. What share of violent crimes against teens occurs on the street, park or playground?

a. 1 of 3 (33%). Almost one-third of violent crimes against teens occur on the street or at the park or playground. An additional 27 per cent occur at school. Young teenagers were most likely to experience robberies and aggravated assaults on a street or in a park but were most likely to be victims of simple assault while in a school building or on school property. Older teenagers were most likely to be victims of all types of violent crime while on a street or in a park. Teenagers in both age groups were most likely to experience crimes of theft in a school building or on school property. Younger teenagers, however, were about three times as likely as older teens to experience theft at school (81 per cent of all vs. 39 per cent for older teens). (Source: *Teenage Victims*)

What steps should be taken to reduce the risk of crime to teens while away from home? Among the steps/behaviours that can help reduce teens' risk of being victims on the street:

- Walk on well-lighted, safe streets at night.
- Do not hitchhike.
- Avoid dangerous shortcuts.
- Do not carry large sums of money.
- Travel with one or more friends.
- This quiz was taken from *Charting Success*, a publication of the Teens, Crime, and the Community programme.

A streetwise guide to having a good time

Information from the Metropolitan Police

Concerts, football matches, events

There's a way of going to crowded events and enjoying yourself without taking unnecessary risks. It involves knowing that you and your property are safe, feeling confident, and taking a little bit of time out to plan ahead. You don't need anything special to become a relaxed, experienced crowd-member. All it takes are:

Friends

You feel more confident and relaxed with people you know. Travel with them if you can, or arrange to meet them at a well-known, public place near the venue. Don't choose the main entrance – it's likely to be a mass of people, all looking for one another. Once you've made contact, try to stay with them. Agree an easily recognisable point inside the venue where you'll meet if you do get separated.

Money

Work out in advance how much money you're going to need. Keep your cash in a secure inside pocket or money belt; if you take a bag, wear it with the strap pulled forward so that the bag itself is under your arm. (Bags slung over people's shoulders are a gift to pickpockets.) Put aside enough money to get you home and carry it separately so that if you are robbed, you won't be stranded. For the same reason, it's a good idea to keep your doorkeys away from your purse.

Walkmans/cameras/accessories

Leave them at home. There'll be people on the look out for what they can steal. If you must take them, make sure they are as secure as your purse or wallet and never put them down. It takes only a split second for someone to take them.

Quick reactions

There's always a buzz of excitement in a crowd; usually it's just part of the atmosphere, but it can sometimes spill over into fights. Trouble can spread quickly. If you see a fight or a nasty situation building, don't stick around to watch. Get away. Notice where police/security are stationed and don't hesitate to report an incident or ask for help.

Sharp eyes

Necessary for checking out souvenirs, tickets or anything else you're offered for sale. There are always things to buy at these events, and it's smart to have a hard look at the goods before you part with your money. Many will be fine, but don't let yourself be conned or ripped off with rubbish. Be very, very careful about buying tickets from touts – there are a lot of forgeries around – and don't pay more than you can sensibly afford.

Steady legs

It's very rare that a crowd panics but if it happens, don't waste time trying to pick up anything you drop: the most important thing is to stay on your feet. If you feel the crowd begin to push in one direction, don't try to fight against the flow – go with it. When things settle down, try to move away to a safer area.

Emergency exits

These are useful things to notice at any time and of course, they're vital in an emergency. They'll be clearly marked, usually in red lettering on white. Take time out to work out how you would get away if you had to.

Substances

It's illegal for you to take them. Don't be confident about your ability to 'handle' drugs. Drugs are dangerous and you need to stay in control. You enjoy an event more if you know what's going on around you.

The trip home

Arranging the trip home is one of the tricks the experienced crowd member soon learns. Nothing can spoil an outing more than being stranded after it's over, along with a mass of other cold and increasingly fed-up people. Find out when the event is going to end and what buses or trains will be running afterwards. They'll be crowded so leave the venue quickly and go straight to the transport. You may even get a seat.

Parties

Even the best parties can go badly wrong. All the ways we have suggested for staying safe and problem-free at events also apply to parties.

And if you're being taken to a party held by someone you don't know, find out about it in advance. Where is it? Who else do you know who's going? How will you get there and back? Let someone know where you're going to be – it gives you and them confidence.

In a private home, there won't be emergency exits, but you can notice where the doors are and the telephone. Keep your money on you, rather than leaving it in your jacket.

Like organised events, parties have moods. Trust yourself to pick up on them. Even if you just feel uncomfortable but can't say why, then leave.

At the club/ in the park/ on the street...

You're walking down a quiet street, going to your friend's place. You're wearing your personal stereo. The quickest way is through the car park, and you're just starting to go in when you see a group of people leaning against a car, chatting. You've got no reason to suspect them of doing anything wrong, but you feel wary. It will only take ten seconds to cross the car park.

What do you do?

Turn round and take another, more public route. Don't go into the car park. What's the point of looking for trouble? Take your headphones off and put them in your pocket – as long as you're wearing them, you can't hear what's going on around you and you're advertising the fact that you've got something to steal. Always walk away from the building line of a street. You do not know who is standing in the next shop doorway. Give yourself a chance to run away by putting some distance between them and yourself. Always choose the the busiest and brightly lit route home even if it is longer. Think of your safety first.

Remember

- To have a good time in your free time.
- Keep with your group.
- Think about where you're going – is it smart to take your valuable possessions with you?
- Take well-lit and well-used routes.
- Carry money securely.
- Keep your headphones off when you're alone.
- Walk confidently – head up, arms swinging – even if you don't feel it.
- Trust your instincts and don't do anything you don't want to.

If you are worried, frightened or think you may be in danger, call 999

© *Metropolitan Police Service (MPS)*

Youth questions and answers

Information from the Metropolitan Police

Are these people breaking the law, yes or no?

1. Pete is having a party in his flat. There is a lot of booze and some people are smoking cannabis. Pete is not smoking himself but knows it is going on. Is Pete breaking the law?

Answer: If Pete knows his flat is being used to take drugs and does nothing about it he could be prosecuted under section 8 of the Misuse of Drugs Act 1971.

2. David smokes cannabis but claims he is immune from prosecution because he is a Rastafarian. His religion approves of 'Ganja'. Is he breaking the law?

Answer: Membership of a religious group does not override the Drug Laws. He is at risk of arrest for being in possession of a controlled drug.

3. Richard and his friend put their money together to buy some cannabis. Richard takes the money and buys it from a man he knows. When he returns he shares the cannabis out with his friends. Can Richard be arrested for being a drug dealer?

Answer: Yes, he can be arrested for dealing drugs. Although there is no intention to profit personally, he still commits the offence of supplying drugs to his friends.

4. Tony and Jane are 17 and go into their local pub. They buy a pint of bitter and a pint of lager. The pub gets raided by the police. Can Jane and Tony be arrested?

Answer: Yes and No. Under-age drinking of alcohol in a licensed premises is an offence which could lead to them being 'summoned' to go to court by letter. If they refuse to give their name and address they can be arrested. (The publican could also be prosecuted.)

5. Kal is 14 and she goes into her local shop to buy some cigarettes. Is she breaking the law?

Answer: The shopkeeper is

breaking the law not Kal. Kal is being stupid with her health. Not all boys like kissing ashtrays!

6. Gary and Paula are 15 and sitting in the park sniffing glue. Are they breaking the law?

Answer: No, it is not illegal to purchase or use solvents (glue or gas). It is only illegal for the shopkeeper to sell it to those under 18 years. Police officers will remove any glue sniffers to a police station as a 'Place of Safety' to be seen by our doctor and await the arrival of your parents. The Social Services will also be informed. If you are acting disorderly you will be arrested under the Public Order Act 1986. Do not sniff glue or gas because you can DIE. When you get 'high' you could be sick as the solvents do not taste nice. The danger is that you drown on your own vomit. I have seen it and it is horrible.

7. Karen finds a purse on the pavement containing £300. If she keeps it is she breaking the law?

Answer: Yes, this is called theft by finding and she could be arrested. What she must do is take it to a police station. If nobody claims it after four weeks she is given it back.

8. If you are shouting and swearing in a busy street are you breaking the law?

Answer: Yes. If a police officer asks you to stop and you ignore him you can be arrested for Disorderly Behaviour under section of the 5 Public Order Act 1986.

9. John is going shopping. In his pocket he has a stanley knife which has a lockable 2cm blade. Is he breaking the law?

Answer: Yes, you are not allowed to carry any knife that locks in place. It does not matter how big or small the blade is. You can be arrested for carrying it.

10. Jake is going to the chip shop and is carrying in his pocket a Swiss Army penknife with a 2-inch blade. Is he breaking the law?

Answer: No, so long as he has not got it for his own protection. You can carry a pocket knife which has a blade under 3 inches so long as it does not lock into position. If you are a Scout you could be breaking the law if you wear a sheath knife.

© *Metropolitan Police Service (MPS)*

Fit children 'less likely' to offend

By Nick Hopkins

Children who have health problems are far more likely to be drawn into crime than those who are fit, a report claims today.

Drawing on the results of previous studies on alcohol and drug abuse to show the links, the National Association for the Care and Resettlement of Offenders makes a series of recommendations, which, it says, could cut youth crime.

They include national minimum standards for school meals, drug education at primary schools, improved health screening for people with learning difficulties, and the creation of an agency where children can refer themselves for help and advice.

The 24-page report, *Children, Health and Crime*, also calls for alcohol and drugs education to be included as a core element of the national curriculum.

Research shows that 50% of boys and a third of girls sentenced to

There is 'a mutually enforcing relationship between delinquent behaviour and unhealthy lifestyles'

custody suffer from mental illness, and many young offenders abuse drink and drugs.

More than 40% were drunk or had been drinking when they committed a crime, and 37% of offenders were judged to have a serious problem with either drink or drugs.

The report accepts other issues are involved, including poor parenting and truancy. But it concludes that there is 'a mutually enforcing relationship between delinquent behaviour and unhealthy lifestyles'.

The report says the key to cutting youth crime is the promotion of healthy living and the provision of support agencies.   © *The Guardian June, 1999*

Straw urges public to act on the spot against child crime

Jack Straw, the Home Secretary, yesterday called on members of the public to follow his example of intervening to stop acts of vandalism and low-level crime by children.

Mr Straw, who has made several citizen's arrests, said he wanted to see an end to the 'walk on by' society. In a speech to the Social Market Foundation he said: 'If we want to live our lives free from crime, we must recognise that we all have a responsibility to help reduce it.'

He said that turning a blind eye to youngsters engaged in vandalism was to ignore a shared duty to ensure that they grew up to be responsible members of society. Mr Straw cited his own experience 10 days ago when, as he waited for a train at Blackburn station, he saw a teenage boy spitting over a parapet on to a walkway. Mr Straw said: 'I went up to him and said "Look, can you imagine what it's like to be walking up there and being spat on?" and he gave me quite a lot of lip but after a while he calmed down.'

It is not the first time Mr Straw has decided to 'have a go'. He chased a mugger after seeing him target a young boy at the Oval

*By George Jones,
Political Editor*

underground station, near his London home, in 1982. He caught the man and handed him over to the authorities. On another occasion in London, he and another man wrestled a 65-year-old woman's mugger to the ground, tying his legs together until police arrived.

> **He said that turning a blind eye to youngsters engaged in vandalism was to ignore a shared duty to ensure that they grew up to be responsible members of society**

In his Blackburn constituency, Mr Straw pursued a 20-year-old burglar, catching him 100 yards from a police station. In 1997, after becoming Home Secretary, Mr Straw took his 17-year-old son to a police station after he was accused of selling a small amount of cannabis to a tabloid newspaper reporter. His son was eventually cautioned.

Mr Straw said everybody had to realise that they had a role to play in confronting the low-level disorder and disrespect that led to more serious crime. He said: 'Somewhere along the line, we as a society started to feel that what other people's children got up to in public was none of their business. It was a job solely for their parents or teachers or police officers.

'Today, how many of us, seeing a group of 11- or 12-year-olds vandalising a phone box or picking on a younger child, would actually intervene? Yet if we do not, who else will? And this is not just about young people as offenders – but as victims, too. If we ignore young people when they are causing trouble, we start to ignore them when they are in danger.'

But the National Association for the Care and Resettlement of Offenders said that although the whole community had a responsibility for tackling youth crime, it was risky for people to intervene even in a low-level crime situation.

Beat the burglar

Make your home more secure

Make it difficult for the burglar

Most burglaries are committed by opportunist thieves. In two out of ten burglaries they don't even have to use force – they get in through an open door or window.

Look at your home through the burglar's eyes – are there places where they could break in unseen? Have you fitted strong locks on your doors and windows? Would they have to make a lot of noise by breaking glass?

Reduce the risk of burglary happening to you by making sure you've taken these simple precautions.

For a relatively small outlay you could make your home more secure and buy peace of mind into the bargain.

Windows

A third of burglars get in through a back window.

Easily visible locks may deter some thieves, because a window lock forces the thief to break the glass and risk attracting attention. DIY shops sell inexpensive key-operated locks to fir all kinds of window.

- Fit key-operated window locks to all downstairs windows, those which can't be seen from the street and easily accessible upstairs windows, e.g. those above a flat roof or by a drainpipe.
- Even small windows such as skylights or bathroom fanlights need locks – a thief can get through any gap larger than a human head.

Remember to remove keys from locked windows and to keep them out of sight in a safe place.

- Louvre windows are especially vulnerable because the slats can be removed easily from the frame. Glue the slats in place with an epoxy resin, and fit a special

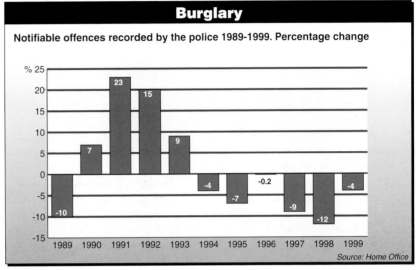

Burglary

Notifiable offences recorded by the police 1989-1999. Percentage change

Source: Home Office

louvre lock. Better still replace them with fixed glass.
- If you are replacing windows – consider laminated glass.
- As a last resort, consider fitting security grilles to vulnerable windows – many DIY shops now sell decorative wrought-iron grilles.

Casement locks make it impossible to open windows without the correct key. Fanlight locks have a metal bolt to secure the metal arm used to open and close the window.

Lighting

Good lighting can deter a thief.

Some exterior lights have an infra-red sensor that switches the light on for a few moments when it detects something in its range. Sensors can be bought separately to convert an existing outdoor light into a security one.

Look in when you're out

Most burglaries happen when a house or flat is empty, so:

- Use time switches – available from DIY shops – to turn on lights, radios and other appliances when you're out.

- Don't tempt the thief – keep all valuable items out of sight.
- Don't advertise your absence when you're on holiday, or even when out at work or shopping. Most burglars will only tackle an empty house.
- If you can, get a friend or neighbour to look after your home when you're away, by collecting your post, drawing your curtains at night and generally making the place look lived in. And be prepared to do the same for them.

Burglar alarms

Visible burglar alarms make burglars think twice.

There are many systems on the market, ranging from cheaper DIY alarms to more sophisticated alarms costing hundreds of pounds. Easily installable 'wire-free' alarms are now available whereby sensors fitted around the house transmit radio detection signals to a control system. These systems usually take 3-4 hours to fit. Wired alarms are cheaper but take longer – around a day – to install.

- Get specialist advice and a number of quotes.
- Consult your insurance company for companies they recommend

before deciding which best suits your needs. The system should meet BS4737 (professionally installed) or BS6707 (DIY).

Remember, a badly-fitted alarm can create problems in itself. Don't install a DIY system unless you have the electrical knowledge and practical skill to do so.

If you live in a flat

The most vulnerable part of your flat is likely to be the front door.

- Replace a weak door. It should be as strong as the main entry door.
- Fit hinge bolts which stop the door being pulled off its hinges.
- Fit a steel strip to the door frame to strengthen it.
- Consider having a door telephone entry system installed. Never 'buzz' open the door for strangers or hold the door open for someone who is arriving as you are leaving.

Spare key

- Never leave a spare key in a convenient hiding place such as under the doormat or in a flower pot – a thief will look there first.
- If you're moving into a new house, consider changing the back and front door locks – other people may have keys that fit.

Side passages

- Fit a strong, lockable, high gate across the passage to stop a thief getting to the back of the house where they can work undisturbed. If you share an alleyway with a neighbour, ask their permission and for help with the cost.

Garages and sheds

Often full of expensive tools ideal for breaking into the rest of the house – and often left unlocked.

- Never leave a garage or garden shed unlocked, especially if it has a connecting door to the house – a thief could get in and work on the inner door in privacy.
- Fit shed and garage doors with a strong padlock and make sure that they are solid enough not to be kicked in.
- Lock ladders inside the garage or shed to stop a thief using them to reach inaccessible windows. If there is no room inside, chain or

padlock them horizontally to a sturdy bracket on an outside wall.

Gates and fences

- Check for weak spots where a thief could get in – a low or sagging fence, or a back gate with weak lock.
- A thorny hedge along the boundary can act as a deterrent. But make sure that the front of the house is still visible to passers-by so that a burglar can't work unseen.

Doors

Secure all doors

If your front and back doors are not secure, neither is your home.

- Make sure the doors and frames are strong and in good condition. Doors should be made of solid core construction – 44mm thick.
- Glass panels on or around the door are especially vulnerable, so replace them with laminated glass.
- Fit back and front doors with a five-lever mortice deadlock – and use it.
- Fit all exterior doors – top and bottom – with bolts. Remember to fit all security devices with strong screws or bolts.
- Get specialist advice on fitting locks to patio doors.

- Fit both french doors, top and bottom, with a security mortice lock and mortice bolt.

Patio doors should have special locks fitted top and bottom unless they already have a multi-locking system.

If you're thinking of buying PVCu or metal-framed windows or doors, make sure that they come with good built-in locks and a fitted chain, which can be very difficult and expensive to add retrospectively.

Look in your telephone directory for the names of local locksmiths who are members of the Master Locksmiths' Association.

Rim latch

Most front doors are fitted with a rim latch which locks automatically when the door is closed but can be opened again from the inside without a key.

For extra protection you should consider installing the following:

Automatic deadlock

This locks automatically when the door is closed, but when locked externally with a key, cannot be opened from the inside.

Chains

These help you to speak with strangers at the door without letting them in.

Remember, if in doubt, keep them out.

Buy a chain and use it every time you open the door.

Mortice deadlock

Fit a five-lever deadlock about a third of the way up the door. One kitemarked to at least BS3621 should satisfy most insurance requirements.

A deadlock with a key, so a thief can't smash a nearby panel to open the door from the inside; if the thief gets into the property through a window they can't carry your property out through the door.

Hinges

Check that the door hinges are sturdy and secured with strong, long screws.

For added security fit hinge bolts. These are inexpensive and help to reinforce the hinge side of a door against the use of force.

Door viewers
Enable you to identify callers before opening the door.

Letterboxes
Never hang a spare key inside the letterbox – an obvious place that a thief will check.

Consider fitting a letterbox cage which prevents thieves from putting their hand through the letterbox and trying the locks from the inside.

Don't forget
Postcode your property
In only 9% of cases where something has been stolen is property returned.

Marked property can deter burglars because it's harder for a thief to sell and can help the police to return it if found.

- Mark items with indelible identification – showing your postcode and the number of your house or flat or the first two letters of its name – using a permanent etching tool or an ultra-violet marking pen. Only use UV marking when other methods would reduce the value of the object, because the mark can fade.

Take pictures of all valuable items like jewellery and silverware and write down the serial numbers of your TV, video, hi-fi, home computer and camera equipment, to help the police identify them should they be recovered. If you have many valuable items, fit a safe.

Ask your local police station for 'postcoded property' stickers to display in the front and back windows of your house.

Insurance
Are you fully insured? Insurance will relieve you of the financial worry of replacing stolen goods and many insurance companies offer reduced premiums for people with good home security. Ask the firm if it minds which systems you buy.

Smoke detectors
With all security, consideration must be given to the risk of fire and means of escape. Fit a smoke detector – a minimum of one per floor – installed to the manufacturer's instructions to BS5446 Part 1.

Be a good neighbour
If you see anyone acting suspiciously in your neighbourhood, call the police. Join a Neighbourhood Watch Scheme – there are now over 130,000 in this country. Anyone can start up a Watch – call your police for details.

If you are burgled
A secure home will reduce the chance of you getting burgled. But, if you get home and notice signs of a break-in:
- Don't go in or call out – the intruder could still be inside.
- Go to a neighbour's to call the police.

Crime prevention advice
All police forces have officers trained in crime prevention – contact your local station for advice.

Some forces can arrange surveys of your home or business premises and recommend security improvements. This is a popular service – if there's a waiting list you may be sent an information pack so you can do your own survey.

© Crown Copyright

Property offences

The number of property offences fell by 1.1 per cent, with 4.3 million offences recorded during 1998/99. This is the sixth consecutive financial year decrease in property offences, which have fallen from a record number of 5.3 million during 1992/93.

There were decreases in many offence groups within property crime; however fraud and forgery, arson and the theft from the person groups showed large increases.

Burglary offences make up 22 per cent of all recorded property crimes. During 1998/99 domestic burglaries fell by 5.7 per cent (473,000 offences were recorded), with non-domestic burglaries falling by 1.6 per cent to 479,800 offences. Despite falls during the past six years, the total number of burglaries recorded is still 19 per cent higher than ten years ago.

Thefts made up 51 per cent of all recorded property crimes. During 1998/99 recorded thefts fell by 0.9 per cent to 2,191,500 thefts – the sixth consecutive financial year fall. However, theft offences are still 12 per cent higher than ten years ago.

Offences of thefts from the person rose by 8.9 per cent to 63,100 during 1998/99 – more than reversing the small fall recorded during the previous year. Thefts from shops increased by 2.9 per cent to 282,000. Thefts of pedal cycles decreased for the seventh financial year running – the 10.6 per cent fall reduced the total to 128,600 offences.

Fraud and forgery offences rose by 27.5 per cent. This is after the exclusion of the effect of the new counting rules, which now allows the recording of unreported cheque and credit-card fraud offences that are discovered by the police in subsequent investigation. In some forces the change in counting rules has coincided with a review of recording practices for cheque and credit-card fraud offences. These reviews have resulted in more reported offences being recorded, thus causing increases in recorded offences that are not directly attributable to the new rules.

There were 879,600 criminal damage offences recorded in 1998/99, a fall of 3.2 per cent on the previous year. This total contained 47,300 arson offences and 3,300 threats to commit criminal damage. Forty-three per cent of the remaining criminal damage was against vehicles, 27 per cent against dwellings, 19 per cent against other buildings, and 11 per cent against other 'objects' such as bus shelters and post boxes.

- The above information is from the Home Office document *Recorded Crime Statistics*.

© Home Office
October, 1999

Widdecombe would give homeowners legal right to use force

**By Polly Newton,
Political Staff**

Homeowners should be allowed to use force to protect their property without fear of prosecution, Ann Widdecombe said yesterday.

The shadow home secretary suggested that the Conservatives would give householders greater freedom to fight off intruders. She told the Blackpool audience: 'I believe that it is every citizen's right, within reasonable and sensible limits, to defend themselves and their property against attack without fearing a penalty in law.'

'Parents should have the right – again, within reasonable and sensible limits – to prevent their children from associating with people who might lead them astray', said the shadow home secretary. Her comments, which earned loud applause, follow the case of the Norfolk farmer who is facing a murder charge after allegedly shooting dead a young burglar caught on his property.

In another recent incident, a father was detained by police for attempting to restrain his teenage daughter when she wanted to meet friends of whom he disapproved.

Miss Widdecombe attacked Jack Straw, the Home Secretary, for a series of failures since the general election. Crime had risen for the first time in five years, police recruitment had fallen and record numbers of bogus asylum seekers were entering Britain, she said.

The Conservatives would restore police numbers to their pre-election level and free officers for crime prevention and detection work by relieving them of certain responsibilities such as escorting wide loads on motorways. Miss Widdecombe said the party would also reintroduce the list of 'safe countries' from which asylum seekers could be put on an immigration fast track.

'Where they fail to make a case, they will be turned around very quickly,' she said. Such a step was not only in the interests of taxpayers or people living in areas like Dover or Folkestone, 'it is overwhelmingly in the interests of the genuine asylum seeker fleeing terrible persecution'.

> **'I believe that it is every citizen's right to defend themselves and their property against attack without fearing a penalty in law'**

Miss Widdecombe also criticised the Government's prisons policy, which she said allowed some offenders to leave jail after serving a fraction of their sentence. A Conservative government would ensure that criminals served the sentence they were given in court.

She said: 'That doesn't necessarily mean that everybody's going to serve twice the sentence they serve at the moment. But it does mean that the sentence will be transparent and will be certain and will have meaning and what is more the judges and magistrates will decide whether or not to take into account time spent on remand.'

The Tories would ensure that prisoners spent their time in jail productively, she added. Rehabilitation for offenders was 'not some sort of soft, liberal, wet option but a crucial measure of public protection'.

Miss Widdecombe said the Tories would pay greater attention to the needs of victims of crime, who would be given the statutory right to have a named police officer and Crown Prosecution Service employee dealing with their case.

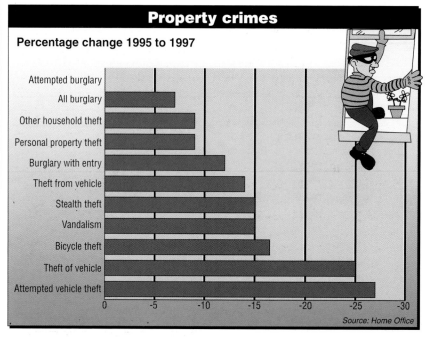

Property crimes

Percentage change 1995 to 1997

- Attempted burglary
- All burglary
- Other household theft
- Personal property theft
- Burglary with entry
- Theft from vehicle
- Stealth theft
- Vandalism
- Bicycle theft
- Theft of vehicle
- Attempted vehicle theft

0 -5 -10 -15 -20 -25 -30

Source: Home Office

Peace of mind while you're away

Advice on keeping your home secure

Everyone needs a holiday some time. And however much you like your home, there's nothing like a change of surroundings.

But you want to come home and find everything as you left it. Four out of five burglaries occur when a house or flat is empty, so don't advertise that you're away on holiday.

Plan ahead

The checklist below will help you to keep your home secure. Read it now so that you so can plan ahead. Then tick off the items just before you go.

Help from your neighbours

It's a good idea to get help from your neighbours. All you have to do is fill in the card below and give it to a friend or neighbour. It asks them to keep an eye on your home while you're away.

You could also ask them to collect post left in the letterbox, sweep up leaves, even mow the lawn and generally make the place look lived in.

You can repay the favour by doing the same for them. Warn your key-holding neighbour not to put your surname, address or even your house number on your keys in case they fall into the wrong hands.

Is there a Neighbourhood Watch scheme where you live? It could help you keep your home secure while you're away, and has many other crime prevention and community benefits.

Checklist

- Help reduce the risk of your home being broken into by taking some simple home-security measures. The free booklet *Your Practical Guide to Crime Prevention* has over a hundred tips on preventing crime, available from your local police station or write to Home Office, PO Box 999, Sudbury, Suffolk CO10 6FS.

- Leave small valuable items, like jewellery, on deposit at the bank, or consider installing a small floor safe. Don't lock internal doors or

> Dear neighbour,
> Please be a good neighbour and look after my house while I'm away. Check doors and windows (every day, if possible). Push newspapers and letters right through the letter-box. Make sure no milk or other deliveries are left on the step. And if you see or hear anything suspicious, please don't hesitate to dial 999 and ask for the police.
> Signed: ....
> Home address:...............................
>   Thank you for your help – I'll look after your home while you are away.
> - I will be away from . . .
> - Returning on . . .
> - Holiday address(es), dates and telephone numbers
> - Holiday company telephone
> - Car make, colour and registration
> - Please keep this card in a safe place – thank you. (If you have my spare key, please don't mark it with my surname, address, house number or anything similar.)

desks – they may be forced if someone does break in.

- Mark any other valuable items with your postcode followed by the house number or the first two letters of the house name. Then if they are stolen and later found, the police can identify and return them to you. Use the right security marker – DIY shops sell property-marking kits. Ask your local crime prevention officer for 'postcoded property' warning stickers to display in the front and back windows of your house. Also take photos of all valuable items. This is particularly important for those which may be unsuitable for marking.
- Arrange for pets to be properly looked after.
- Cut the lawn before you go.
- Cancel deliveries of milk, news-papers, etc., discreetly – don't announce your departure to a shop full of people. Only tell people who need to know you're going away.
- Make sure your house looks occupied. Closed curtains in the daytime make it look as if no one is home. It is worthwhile to get automatic time-switches to

switch lights – and a radio – on and off in downstairs rooms.

- Don't leave valuable items like TVs, videos or hi-fi visible through windows.
- Lock the garage and shed with proper security locks, after putting all your tools safely away so they cannot be used to break into your house. If you have to leave a ladder out, put it on its side and lock it to a secure fixture with a 'close-shackle' padlock and a heavy-duty chain.
- Don't have your home address showing on your luggage for the outward journey. Put this only on the inside of your cases.
- Finally, lock all outside doors and windows. If you have a burglar alarm, make sure it is set – and that you have told the police who the key-holder is.

And just before you actually set off, it's worth allowing a quiet couple of minutes on the doorstep to check you've done all you had to do and taken everything you need with you.

Practical ways to crack crime

Information from Neighbourhood Watch

Crime, as we are all aware, has been a growing problem all over the world in the last 30 years. But we are not powerless against crime. Much is being done – and more can be done – to reverse the trend. You can play a part in it.

The first step towards preventing crime is understanding its nature. Most crime is against property, not people. Most is not carried out by professionals; nor is it carefully planned. Property crimes thrive on the opportunity. They are often committed by adolescents and young men, the majority of whom stop offending as they grow older. Peak ages for offending are 15 to 18. Also, and not surprisingly, the risk of crime varies greatly depending on where you live. This reliance by criminals on the easy opportunity is the key to much crime prevention. Motor cars, for example, are a sitting target for the criminal.

Expensive, attractive and mobile, they are often left out on the street for long periods at a time. The police estimate that 70-90% of car crimes result from easy opportunity. Surveys have shown that approximately 1 in 5 drivers do not always bother to secure their cars by looking all the doors and shutting all the windows.

It's the same story with our homes. In approximately 30% of domestic burglaries, the burglar simply walks in without using force; the householder has left a door unlocked or a window open. If opportunities like this did not exist, criminals would have a much harder time. The chances are that many crimes would not be committed at all, which would in turn release more police time for tackling serious crime.

There are many ways to be involved in crime prevention in the area where you live or work

Of course, the primary responsibility for coping with crime rests with the police and courts. But there are many ways you can help reverse the trend. So if you care about improving the quality of life for yourself, your family and the community, read on . . .

Your home

Eight out of ten burglaries are not committed by professional criminals. And in three burglaries out of ten, a thief does not even have to use force to get in – a door or a window has been left open. Thieves like easy opportunities. Help reduce the risk of your home being broken into by taking some simple home-security measures.

Your community

There is a lot you can do outside your home and family to help prevent crime. There are many ways to be involved in crime prevention in the area where you live or work. Find out what role you could play in improving the quality of life for yourself and others.

School Watch

Protecting our children

There can be no denying that amongst the most vulnerable of our society are our children and they are most at risk travelling to and returning home from school.

They are at risk not only from the sheer volume of traffic if they need to cross busy roads but, more importantly, they are at risk from the potential child abductor or molester, those of our society who wait outside or near schools for a solitary and vulnerable child, whether boy or girl, and attempt to entice that lone child to go with them and, far too often, force them against their will.

It is the responsibility of all, the schools themselves, the police, the local authority, the Education Welfare Department of the local authority and parents, to work together to ensure, as far as they are able, the safety and welfare of our children.

A School Watch system is simple in its concept but effective in reducing the risks to children and once in place takes very little effort and can be operated within existing resources.

An effective scheme depends on all taking an active part and on information received being circulated to all schools in the shortest possible time. This is achieved by the telephone ring-round or pyramid system, where the top school telephones two schools below and each of those schools telephones two schools below them and so on until all schools within the system have been informed of any message that is important or vital to the safety of the children.

This is only a guide and the completed system would depend on how many schools there are in any individual area. Ideally there should be a maximum of between 15 and 20 schools in each group. It is also important that you try and keep them as closely aligned to their old partnership groups as possible.

I have found through experience that it is much the best idea to use the Education Welfare Department of the local authority as the central link for the system, they through the very nature of their job need to be kept informed of any incident that has come to notice.

A School Watch system is simple in its concept but effective in reducing the risks to children

There should be a dedicated School Watch Officer appointed by the local police who's responsibility it would be to assess any information received whether from a school, parent or child and then decide on the level of circulation.

Once the level of circulation has been decided, whether to circulate to particular groups or all groups within the system, the Education Welfare Department is informed and it is they who initiate the system by telephoning the top school of each of the school groups that that message or information needs to be circulated to, those schools then telephone the two schools below them on the list and so on until all schools have been informed of that message or information.

It is also advisable that a School Watch descriptive form be designed and a supply of these given to all schools in the system. Each school then, on receipt of a School Watch message, completes one of these forms so that consistency is maintained and valuable information like the description of any suspect is not lost or more importantly does not become distorted or altered as it is passed through the system.

Once the framework has been decided and agreed on by all involved it is advisable that some form of user's guide be published and circulated to all involved so that good and correct practices can be maintained throughout. A flow chart can be designed to assist all in the general operation of the system.

This advice is based on a very successful School Watch system currently in operation by Edmonton and Enfield Police Divisions, North London, and the Watch Liaison Officer Len Priestley can be contacted by e-mail (len@crimeweb.org) for any further advice or help.

© *Neighbourhood Watch on the Internet*

Personal safety

Information from the Crime Prevention Initiative at the Home Office

The chances that you, or a member of your family, will be a victim of violent crime is low. Violent crimes are still comparatively rare and account for a very small part of recorded crime. Nevertheless, many people are frightened that they, or someone close to them, will be the victim of a violent attack.

The best way to minimise the risk of attack is by taking sensible precautions. Most people already do this as part of their everyday lives, often without realising it. You may already be aware of some of the suggestions listed below, but some may be new to you, and you may find them useful. They seem particularly relevant to women, but if you are a man, don't stop reading or turn the page. You can act positively to contribute towards women's safety, as well as reducing the risk of assault yourself.

How can you stay safe at home?

Make sure your house or flat is secure. Always secure outside doors. Fit barrel locks top and bottom. If you have to use a key, keep it nearby – you may need to get out quickly in the event of fire.

If other people such as previous tenants could still have keys that fit, change the locks. Don't give keys to workmen or tradesmen, as they can easily make copies.

If you wake to hear the sound of an intruder, only you can decide how best to handle the situation. You may want to lie quietly to avoid attracting attention to yourself, in the hope that they will leave. Or you may feel more confident if you switch on the lights and make a lot of noise by moving about. Even if you're on your own, call out loudly to an imaginary companion: most burglars will flee empty-handed rather than risk a confrontation. Ring the police as soon as it's safe for you to do so. A telephone extension in your bedroom will make you feel more secure as it allows you to call the police immediately, without alerting the intruder.

> ### The best way to minimise the risk of attack is by taking sensible precautions

Draw your curtains after dark and if you think there is a prowler outside dial 999.

Use only your surname and initials in the telephone directory and on the doorplate. That way a stranger won't know whether a man or a woman lives there.

If you see signs of a break-in at your home, like a smashed window or open door, don't go in. The burglar may be inside. Go to a neighbour and call the police.

If you are selling your home, don't show people around on your own. Ask your estate agent to send a representative with anyone who wants to view your house.

When you answer the phone, simply say 'hello'; don't give your number. If the caller claims to have a wrong number, ask him or her to repeat the number required. Never reveal any information about yourself to a stranger and never say you are alone in the house.

If you receive an abusive or threatening phone call, put the receiver down beside the phone, and walk away. Come back a few minutes later and replace the receiver; don't listen to hear if the caller is still there. Don't say anything – an emotional reaction is just what the caller wants. This allows the caller to say what he or she wants to say, without causing distress to you.

If the calls continue, tell the police and the operator and keep a record of the date, time and content of each phone call. This may help the authorities trace the caller.

© Home Office

Personal possessions

Information from the Crime Prevention Initiative at the Home Office

A thief only needs a moment to make off with your valuables. Your coat hung up in a restaurant, your briefcase beside your chair, even your cheque book and cheque card left on the table while you pay the bill . . . all are vulnerable if you look away for a second. So try to be careful at all times.

Money and plastic cards

Don't make it easy for pickpockets. Carry your wallet in an inside pocket, preferably one which can be fastened, not your back pocket. If someone bumps into you in a crowd, see if you still have your wallet or purse.

Cash is a favourite target for thieves, so try to avoid carrying large amounts. When on holiday abroad, take travellers' cheques.

If your credit card is stolen, tell the card company immediately. Keep the number handy. If you delay reporting the loss, it could lead to a crime being committed in your name, as a thief could make fraudulent use of your card. Thieves can use credit cards for over-the-counter and telephone purchases.

Always keep your cheque card separate from your cheque book; a thief needs both to write a cheque.

Never carry the personal identification number (PIN) with your cash-dispensing cards. Always memorise your number, and never disclose it, not even to bank staff or close friends.

Sign new plastic cards as soon as they arrive, and cut up old ones when they expire.

The Association for Payment Clearing Services, through its Card Watch campaign, offers practical advice on how to look after your plastic cards.

Handbags

Never let your handbag out of your sight. On public transport, keep hold of it, with the clasp or zip shut so a thief cannot steal your purse. In the office, keep it in a drawer, or in a corner near you and out of sight. Even in a car, keep it out of sight – if you have the windows open or a door unlocked a thief may reach in when you stop in traffic.

Savings plans and investments

Check whether your life assurance or savings plans documents, if stolen, could be used to cash in the policy. If they can, your bank is the best place to store them.

Passports

Only carry your passport when you need to. Thieves can sell stolen passports, and replacing them takes time and trouble.

Mobile phones

Theft of mobile phones is becoming more and more common but you can help to minimise the risk. Keep your phone out of sight, whether in the car or in the street.

© Home Office

The things you own

Information from the Crime Prevention Initiative at the Home Office

Over a quarter of all recorded crimes are car thefts or thefts from cars – like stereos and mobile phones. It's a problem that affects us all no matter where we live. It diverts much police time and can have serious and sometimes fatal consequences.

Keeping your car safe

If your car is stolen or broken into, it could mean weeks of expensive inconvenience – and losing your no-claims bonus. It may be difficult to protect your car from a determined, professional thief, but most car crime is opportunist and you can put them off with vigilance and relatively cheap security precautions. Don't be wise after the event – take the following tips to turn the tide against car crime.

Basics

Never leave a car door unlocked or a window or sun-roof open – even when just going into a shop for a moment or two. Don't leave any belongings in your car. A thief won't know that a bag or coat doesn't contain something valuable and might break a window to get at it. If you can't take them with you, never leave things on display – lock them in the boot.

Security mark your stereo and if it's removable, always take it with you. Make a note of the serial number and keep it in a safe place.

Don't leave credit cards or cheque books in the glove compartment. 1 in 5 stolen cheque and credit cards are taken from cars.

Never leave your vehicle documents in the car – they could help a thief to sell it.

Remove the ignition key and engage the steering lock – even when parking in your own driveway or garage – and don't forget to lock the garage door.

Always try to park in a well-lit, open location.

Double-check that all car doors, windows, sunroof and boot are locked before leaving it. And put your aerial down to stop it being vandalised.

© Home Office

Safety on the street

Information from the Metropolitan Police Service (MPS)

Here are some streetwise tips for going places easily and safely . . .

- Look confident. Walk with your head up, as if you know where you are going. Keep your hands free – don't walk about with them in your pockets.
- Stay alert. Leave your personal stereos off – they stop you being aware of what's going on around you.
- Keep to well-used roads. Don't use alleyways or short cuts.
- Walk against the flow of traffic, to avoid kerb crawlers.
- In the dark, always stick to well-lit areas.
- If you think you are being followed, cross the road.
- If the person follows you, cross it again. If you are still worried, go at once to a place where there are lots of people, such as a busy shop, and tell someone what's going on. If you can, choose a police officer; if not, go to a family group rather than a single adult and tell them. Always report this kind of thing to the police, even if it's now over. You won't be wasting police time.
- Carry a torch or a whistle, or, better still, a very noisy screech or shrill alarm. They are not expensive and if you carry a personal alarm, you will feel more confident.
- If you start to be frightened, try not to panic. Always try to think around situations.

Public transport – Trains and tubes

Carriages on trains

Go into open ones, where people can walk through, rather than closed compartments. Older British Rail trains have closed compartment carriages marked with a red line on the side above the windows. Avoid these if you are on your own. There will be open-style carriages some-where else on the train. Look for a carriage with several other passengers in it, preferably not all in the same group: it's always safer to have a mix of people around you.

On the Tube (The London Underground)

Go into the front or middle carriages. They are less likely to empty suddenly. Try to choose a carriage which will stop near the exit at the station you are travelling to.

Pickpockets

They like stations and trains, where people are often in a hurry and slightly careless of their possessions. Keep your valuables secure on you – wallets and purses in inside pockets; bags carried forward, with your hand on them.

If you have a heavy bag or box, don't dump it several feet away from you. It will get in the way of other people and may cause an accident. Also, you run a greater risk of having it stolen – it only takes seconds to snatch something when the train stops at a station.

Put big or heavy items on the rack above your head (if there's room) or on an empty seat, where you can keep an eye on them

Rush hours and peak times

When it's crowded and you have to stand, try and find yourself a strap or partition to hold on to, to save getting thrown about.

Be especially careful when you are joining a tube or train from a crowded platform. Also take extra care when getting off crowded trains. Look before you step and 'mind the gap'.

If you are in a crowd and someone is touching you or rubbing against you in a way you don't like, don't put up with it. Either tell them to move back a little or, if you can't face it or aren't sure who's doing it, stick your elbows out to create some more space for yourself. As soon as you can, move to a different part of the carriage.

Even in a thick crowd, if you keep saying 'excuse me' politely but determinedly, people will make way for you. If you are frightened, TELL someone immediately. Choose a family group rather than a single person, and ask if you can stay with them until you feel safe. And always report this kind of thing to the police – even if your information is vague, it will still be useful.

Emergency handles

Notice them. They are marked out in red. If the nearest one is too high, look for another one nearby which

you can reach by climbing on a seat. Tubes have pull-down handles and push buttons. Some BR trains have emergency chains to pull rather than handles. They all have the same effect.

If you find yourself alone in a carriage with people who frighten you, get next to the emergency handle/button/chain, stand straight and let them see you're prepared to use it if there's trouble. Don't be afraid of changing carriages when the train gets in to the next station, if it makes you feel more comfortable.

Platforms on British Rail

If the platform is empty or there are people on it who make you uncomfortable, you can usually stay near the ticket office, or the ticket collector, until the train appears.

Underground platforms

Usually stay near escalators, stairs or lifts, where people will be coming and going. If someone on the platform makes you anxious, go to wherever there are people around who make you feel safe. It's better to miss a tube and get the next one than put yourself at risk.

Always stay in well-lit areas. Many tube station platforms now have Help Points with both emergency and information buttons which you can push. Many also have public telephones.

Buses and coaches

Top deck

Avoid it, especially if you're alone. You're cut off up there. Stay downstairs and if the bus isn't very full, sit as near to the driver as possible. Choose an aisle seat if there's one free.

Bus stops

If you can, do use one in a busy, well-lit place – even if it means a longer queue. If you need to ask someone for directions, go to a transport official if you can. If you're asking strangers, don't tell them the exact address you're going to: give the name of the district or the nearest main road. If they ask how you're going to get home from there, say you'll be met at the bus stop.

Bus stations

Busy, confusing places. Even experienced bus travellers sometimes have problems working out which route they need and where to find it.

Always ask the transport officials and at the information desk – don't worry about repeating your questions if the answers still aren't clear. And when you board the bus, check with the driver that it goes to the right destination. (It means you can relax on the journey, instead of gazing anxiously out of the window wondering if you're heading in the wrong direction.)

Always plan your route before you set off, so you don't have these difficulties.

Taxis

On the street

Choose black cabs rather than mini cabs – unless it's a local minicab company you recognise and trust.

If a car stops without you asking it to and the driver says 'this is a taxi, hop in' – DON'T, even if you can see that it's a black cab. Taxi drivers are only supposed to stop when asked. And minicabs are not supposed to stop in the street at all – they are only ever allowed to pick up pre-arranged bookings.

By phone

Choose a firm whose name you know and trust.

When you're ordering a taxi to come for you, give the address and your surname, and ask the driver to give your name when he arrives. When the taxi comes, wait for him to identify himself. Ask 'who are you for?' rather than 'Are you the taxi for Robertson?'

Ask the firm to quote you a price for the journey over the phone, so you can check that you have enough money.

In the taxi

Always sit in the back, not next to the driver.

Share the taxi with a friend if possible – you'll feel better and it's cheaper.

Don't chat to the driver. If you do talk, keep to general topics and don't give any personal information about yourself.

Travel tips

Plan your journeys – work out how to get there and back.

Put aside enough money for the return fare.

Always let someone know where you're going – preferably your parents or the adult who normally looks after you.

Invest in a phone card and always carry it with you, so if you get stranded you can phone home.

If you don't have a phone card or any money, remember that you can always make a phone call by reversing the charges.

If you lose your fare money or ticket, speak to the driver/guard/ticket officer and explain. Give your name and address and say that the transport company can write to your home for payment. Carry some identification on you to prove that you are genuine.

Never be tempted to walk home alone, especially if it's dark or you are unsure of the area.

Never hitch a lift. You don't know who will stop and you don't want to get into a frightening situation.

If you have no other safe way of getting home, call 999: the police will help you.

If you are worried, frightened or think you may be in danger, call 999.

And if you have had a bad experience, or seen someone else having one, always report it to the police. You will not only be helping yourself, you will also be helping to stop other people getting hurt.

© Metropolitan Police Service (MPS)

Street Watch

Street Watch is a new idea to use your eyes and ears to help the community

Neighbourhood Watch schemes prove how much people can achieve when they go into action against local crime. Street Watch is a separate scheme to take this a step further. In agreement with local police and local people, members work out specific routes and regularly walk their chosen area.

They provide a visible public presence to keep an eye out for crime and to deter it. If Street Watch members spot anything, all they are asked to do is to report it to the police. This practice of alert observation can be integrated with everyday activities.

Schemes must always be set up in consultation with local police who will provide guidance on what members should look out for and how they should behave. It is also vitally important for Street Watch schemes to have the support of the community and to be sensitive to local circumstances.

Street Watch can help to reduce crime because local people know their patch better than anyone and are out and about where it matters.

Being a regular part of the local scene is a great help in making people feel more secure.

Street Watch in action

The people of the small town of Sandwich in East Kent organised their own Street Watch to reduce local crime. The scheme was set up in February 1993 by traders and residents frustrated by the increasing number of burglaries, car thefts and vandalism in the town. It was agreed with the local police that Street Watch members should walk the streets in pairs and anything suspicious would be reported to the police. If they do come across any incidents, the 30 volunteers do not attempt to get involved. They contact the police immediately.

• An extract from the web site www.crime-prevention.org.uk/home_office/partners/swatch/

© Home Office

Unsolved crime cases now on the web

To coincide with the start of the annual Crimestoppers Week on 1st October 1999, a new web site listing unsolved crimes from around the UK has been launched. Designed and hosted by ic24, the free Internet service provider owned by Trinity Mirror Group, the site has over 30 serious crimes including murder, assault, rape and burglary. The site includes the murder of TV personality Jill Dando with an appeal by the Metropolitan Police for more help in their investigation.

Anybody with information about the crimes listed, or any other criminal activity, can call the UK-wide freephone 0800 555 111 number where nobody is asked for their name, but may receive a reward whilst still remaining anonymous. In addition, an experimental system has been introduced on the web site for information to be sent via secure e-mail. All messages are routed through a facility that removes e-mail addresses, so the sender remains anonymous.

Home Secretary Jack Straw has welcomed the new web site: 'Fighting crime is not just down to the government and the police. It is a partnership that requires the support of everyone. Getting information about the activity of criminals to the police is essential if we are to make our communities safer. Crimestoppers is an excellent example of a partnership of the community, the media and the police. The freephone 0800 555 111 number enables people to give information anonymously, and therefore safely if they feel threatened. Thanks to ic24, people who want to help the police can now use the Internet. I encourage web surfers to visit the site and find out about Crimestoppers and, if they know something which could be useful, to respond. Initiatives like this make us all aware of Crimestoppers and the part we can play in solving crimes. I wish the scheme every success.'

Trinity Mirror Group online editor Brendon Parsons said: 'The Internet is a powerful tool and we intend to harness that power for the benefit of ic24 users. This project fits with that aim.'

Crimestoppers has over ten years of success in helping to solve crimes. In that time, 340,000 people have given information leading to the arrest and charge of 32,000 individuals. Property recovered is worth more than £45.5 million. Currently, an average of 14 people are arrested every day thanks to Crimestoppers and this year alone, one person has been charged with murder or attempted murder each week.

The scheme is backed by the independent charity Crimestoppers Trust, whose director is Digby Carter: 'We rely entirely on voluntary income for Crimestoppers,' he said. 'This includes substantial backing from the media to publicise the scheme and the support of ic24 in hosting this new web site will help to raise awareness of how easy it is for anybody to help to fight crime without giving their name.'

• The new web site is at http://www.ic24net/crimestoppers.

*© Crimestoppers Trust
September, 1999*

ADDITIONAL RESOURCES

You might like to contact the following organisations for further information. Due to the increasing cost of postage, many organisations cannot respond to enquiries unless they receive a stamped, addressed envelope.

British Youth Council
65-69 White Lion Street
London, N1 9PP
Tel: 0171 278 0582
Fax: 0171 278 0583
E-mail: mail@byc.org.uk
Web site: www.byc.org.uk
The British Youth Council is the representative body for young people aged 16-25 in the UK. An independent charity, run for and by young people, it represents their views to central and local government, political parties, pressure groups and the media.

Crime Concern
Beaver House
147-150 Victoria Road
Swindon, SN1 3UY
Tel: 01793 863500
Fax: 01793 514 654
Works with local partners to prevent crime and create safer communities. Produces a wide range of crime surveys, reports and briefings specialising in youth crime.

Howard League for Penal Reform
708 Holloway Road
London, N19 3NL
Tel: 0171 281 7722
Fax: 0171 281 5506
E-mail:
howard.league@ukonline.co.uk
Web site: webdotukonline.co.uk/
howard.league
Provides facilities for education, research and critical analysis of the criminal justice and penal system in the UK and Europe. Publish a wide range of useful factsheets.

Joseph Rowntree Foundation (JRF)
The Homestead
40 Water End
York, YO3 6LP
Tel: 01904 629241
Fax: 01904 620072
E-mail: infor@jrf.org.uk
Web site: www.jrf.org.uk/
The Foundation is an independent, non-political body which funds programmes of research and innovative development in the fields of housing, social care and social policy. It publishes its research findings rapidly and widely so that they can inform current debate and practice.

Justice
59 Carter Lane
London, EC4V 5AQ
Tel: 0171 329 5100
Fax: 0171 329 5055
Justice is a legal human rights organisation which aims to improve British justice and works for fair and accessible laws in the UK.

Legal Action Group
242 Pentonville Road
London, N1 9UN
Tel: 0171 833 2931
Fax: 0171 837 6094
E-mail: lag@lag.org.uk
Web site: www.lag.org.uk
Legal Action Group is a national, independent charity which campaigns for equal access to justice for all members of society.

National Association for the Care and Resettlement of Offenders (NACRO)
169 Clapham Road
London, SW9 0PU
Tel: 0171 582 6500
Fax: 0171 735 4666
E-mail: communications@nacro.org.uk
Web site: www.nacro.org/
Their vision is a safer society: where all individuals feel they belong (and human rights and dignity are respected); where resources are used constructively, fairly and effectively to reduce crime (and repair the fabric of society), and where those who do offend are dealt with in ways most likely to reduce further offending, repair relationships and encourage reintegration.

National Youth Agency (NYA)
17-23 Albion Street
Leicester, LE1 6GD
Tel: 0116 285 3700
Fax: 0116 285 3777
E-mail: nya@nya.org.uk
Web site: www.nya.org.uk
The National Youth Agency aims to advance youth work to promote young people's personal and social development, and their voice, influence and place in society. It provides resources to improve work with young people and its management; and secures standards of education and training for youth work.

Prison Reform Trust
The Old Trading House
2nd Floor, 15 Northburgh Street
London, EC1V 0JR
Tel: 0171 251 5070
Fax: 0171 251 5076
Publishes a wide range of publications including *A Look Inside*, a resource pack about prisons. Ask for th
eir publications list.

INDEX

The Internet has been likened to shopping in a supermarket without aisles. The press of a button on a Web browser can bring up thousands of sites but working your way through them to find what you want can involve long and frustrating on-line searches.

And unfortunately many sites contain inaccurate, misleading or heavily biased information. Our researchers have therefore undertaken an extensive analysis to bring you a selection of quality Web site addresses.

★ ★ ★ ★ ★

Metropolitan Police Service
www.met.police.uk
Click on either Education or Crime Prevention for a range of informative articles. The index button reveals all the articles on the site – huge. The News button reveals the Met's 24-hour News Bureau.

National Association for the Care and Resettlement of Offenders (NACRO)
www.nacro.org
NACRO is an independent voluntary organisation working to prevent crime by developing and implementing effective approaches to tackling crime and dealing constructively with offenders. It manages a wide range of projects throughout England and Wales. Its web site is currently under construction but it may be worth checking.

Women in Prison
www.womeninprison.org.uk
Women in Prison (WIP) campaigns for women prisoners. They feel that there is a need for a group committed to effecting change within the women's prison system. Click on Current Issues to see their current views on women in prison issues.

The Home Office
www.homeoffice.gov.uk
A vast site with links to Crime Prevention, Drug Prevention, Police, Prisons and Youth Justice. The Subject Index site is a useful way of navigating the hundreds of articles on this site.

Prison Service
www.hmprisonservice.gov.uk
An impressive site dealing with the major aspects of the prison service. Links include prison life, statistics and a news section.

The Home Office
www.homeoffice.gov.uk/crimprev/cpindex.htm
This is the Crime Prevention site of the Home Office site. Included here is guidance on securing your home and vehicles as well as information on the Neighbourhood Watch and Home Watch schemes. There is also information for businesses on preventing fraud, burglary and theft. The information included is taken from various Home Office booklets and leaflets about crime prevention, all of which are available from the Home Office Publicity Teams.

The Police Federation of England and Wales
www.polfed.org.uk
A useful site for press releases which outline police views on law and order issues.

Crimestoppers
www.crimestoppers-uk.org
Concerned about crime? Want to fight back? Afraid of retribution? Crimestoppers helps you give information about crime in total safety. Crimestoppers Trust was established in 1988 and is the only crime-solving charity. The Trust's role is to co-ordinate the community side of the partnership with the police.

ACKNOWLEDGEMENTS

The publisher is grateful for permission to reproduce the following material.

While every care has been taken to trace and acknowledge copyright, the publisher tenders its apology for any accidental infringement or where copyright has proved untraceable. The publisher would be pleased to come to a suitable arrangement in any such case with the rightful owner.

Chapter One: Current Trends

Big crime rise after five-year fall, © The Independent, August 1999, *The rise of Crime plc*, © The Guardian, September 1999, *Cost of crime in shops hits a record £2bn*, © Telegraph Group Limted, London 1999, *One in ten are victims of car crime*, © The Independent, February 1999, *Countryside in the grip of £100m crime wave*, © Telegraph Group Limted, London 1999, *Fourfold rise in drug offenders over 10 years*, © The Guardian, August 1999, *Drugs and robbery behind record rise in women jailed*, © The Daily Mail, June 1999, *Women in prison double in 6 years*, © Telegraph Group Limited, London 1999, *Crimes in Scotland*, © SACRO, *Public losing confidence in modern police force*, © Telegraph Group Limited, London 1999, *Britain's police then and now*, © Telegraph Group Limited, London 1999, *Recorded crime statistics*, © Crown copyright material is reproduced with the permission of the Controller of Her Majesty's Stationery Office.

Chapter Two: Young Offenders

How children have changed in 50 years, © Telegraph Group Limited, London 1999, *Parents in the dock*, © The Daily Mail, August 1999, *Life becomes more violent for younger men*, © The Independent, August, 1999, *Keeping young people away from crime*, © Crown copyright material is reproduced with the permission of the Controller of Her Majesty's Stationery Office, *Crime spree children get theft therapy*, © The Guardian, April 1999, *Youth courts told to use powers to 'name and shame'*, © The Guardian, April 1999, *Juvenile leads*, © The Guardian, July 1999, *Risk of experiencing crime in Scotland*, © SACRO, *My thoughts on teens, crime and the community in Japan*, © Keiko Suzuki, Japan, *What do you know about teens and crime victims?*, © National Crime Prevention Council, *A streetwise guide to having a good time*, © Metropolitan Police Service (MPS), *Youth questions and answers*, © Metropolitan Police Service (MPS), *Fit children 'less likely' to offend*, © The Guardian, June 1999, *Straw urges public to act on the spot against child crime*, © Telegraph Group Limted, London 1999.

Chapter Three: Crime Prevention

Beat the burglar, © Crown copyright material is reproduced with the permission of the Controller of Her Majesty's Stationery Office, *Burglary*, © Crown copyright material is reproduced with the permission of the Controller of Her Majesty's Stationery Office, *Property offences*, © Crown copyright material is reproduced with the permission of the Controller of Her Majesty's Stationery Office, *Widdecombe would give homeowners legal right to use force*, © Telegraph Group Limited, London 1999, *Property crimes*, © Crown copyright material is reproduced with the permission of the Controller of Her Majesty's Stationery Office, *Peace of mind while you're away*, © Crown copyright material is reproduced with the permission of the Controller of Her Majesty's Stationery Office, *Practical ways to crack crime*, © Crown copyright material is reproduced with the permission of the Controller of Her Majesty's Stationery Office, *School Watch*, © Neighbourhood Watch on the Internet, *Personal safety*, © Crown copyright material is reproduced with the permission of the Controller of Her Majesty's Stationery Office, *Personal possessions*, © Crown copyright material is reproduced with the permission of the Controller of Her Majesty's Stationery Office, *The things you own*, © Crown copyright material is reproduced with the permission of the Controller of Her Majesty's Stationery Office, *Safety on the street*, © Metropolitan Police Service (MPS), *Street Watch*, © Crown copyright material is reproduced with the permission of the Controller of Her Majesty's Stationery Office, *Unsolved crime cases now on the web*, © Crimestoppers Trust, September 1999.

Photographs and illustrations:

Pages 1, 9, 14, 20, 25, 27, 35, 38: Pumpkin House, pages 2, 6, 13, 16, 18, 22, 28, 30, 33, 34, 36: Simon Kneebone.

Craig Donnellan
Cambridge
January, 2000